ECONOMICS

For Every Indian

Akash Kumar grew up in Motihari, Bihar. When he spent a school year in the United States as part of the KL-YES Programme of the US Department of State, he could not stop asking why some places stay poor while others get rich. That question never left. He studied at IIT Madras, led academic programmes for Students For Liberty across South Asia and had a short stint working with the Chief Minister's Office of Maharashtra. He has written for *Hindustan Times*, *Deccan Herald* and *News18*, among others. Today he is co-founder and CEO at Raaz MD, India's first AI-powered digital therapeutics platform for men's health. When not building Raaz or arguing about economic policy, he is usually hunting for a good cup of specialty coffee. Find him on X at @aye_kaash and at akashkumar.co.

Kumar Anand grew up in Saharsa, Bihar. It might explain why two people from small-town Bihar ended up writing a book about why prosperity is so unevenly distributed. Kumar is an economist and public policy professional with over fifteen years of experience working on questions of Indian economic growth, economic history and public policy at organizations including Asianomics Limited, the National Institute of Public Finance and Policy, Free A Billion and the Centre for Civil Society. He has written for publications including *The Hindu*, *Rajasthan Patrika* and the French weekly *Le Point*, among others. He studied economics at the University of Delhi and the Gokhale Institute of Politics and Economics, Pune. Find him on X at @kumaranand and at kumaranand.com.

Advance Praise for the Book

'Akash Kumar and Kumar Anand have written a clear and engaging introduction to the content of economics for the curious reader.'
Professor Vernon L. Smith
Nobel Laureate in Economic Sciences, 2002, and Founder, Economic Science Institute, Chapman University

'Here is a lively, readable, common-sense guide to everything you always wanted to know about economics but were afraid to ask.'
Gurcharan Das
Author and Public Intellectual

'Economics is the study of human behaviour, and helps us understand the world. And yet it is misunderstood as a dismal science. This is a marvellous little book that will open the eyes of every reader, and make them look around with both wonder and clarity. Much needed!'
Amit Varma
Author and Host of The Seen and the Unseen

'Every Indian politician and policy maker should read this book. Akash Kumar and Kumar Anand have brilliantly made sensible economics accessible to ordinary Indians.'
Sadanand Dhume
Senior Fellow, American Enterprise Institute, and Columnist, Wall Street Journal

'Adam Smith for India! This book brings the timeless principles of economics to life through Indian history, markets and policy battles – an indispensable guide to understanding how markets and politics shape India's present and future.'
Professor Alex Tabarrok
Bartley J. Madden Chair in Economics at the Mercatus Center, George Mason University, and Co-author of Marginal Revolution, *One of the World's Most Famous Economics Blogs*

'This book is a delightful reminder that economics is not merely about models and equations, but about the quiet logic underlying everyday life. With wit, charm and an economist's eye for the unseen, Akash Kumar and Kumar Anand turn familiar scenes – street markets, cricket matches, airport snacks and global supply chains – into windows on some of the discipline's most powerful ideas. The result is a book that is both playful and intellectually serious, inviting readers to appreciate the remarkable role of economics in making modern prosperity possible. A lively and thoughtful guide to learning how economists see the world.'

Professor Pravin Krishna
Chung Ju Yung Distinguished Professor of International Economics and Business School of Advanced International Studies, Johns Hopkins University

'This book bridges the vast gap between what economists know and what citizens understand about their own economy with clarity, wit and a storyteller's flair. A rare book that makes economics both illuminating and engaging. It deserves to be read by every student and every curious citizen.'

Professor Umakant Dash
Vice Chancellor, Gokhale Institute of Politics and Economics, Pune

'*Economics: For Every Indian* is a refreshing addition to the vast library on economics. Rather than focusing on the apparent precision of maths, models and formulas, Kumar and Anand make economics comprehensible for normal people. They explain how markets and economies work using simple, easy-to-grasp language and do so with illustrative examples and references to Indian society and culture to make the reader feel at home. The result is an effective antidote to the economic illiteracy that plagues both India and the world.'

Professor Per Bylund
Johnny D. Pope Chair, School of Entrepreneurship, Oklahoma State University

'This book is insightful as well as enjoyable, a rare combination. Akash Kumar and Kumar Anand have used simple examples from everyday life to write this excellent guide to the economic way of thinking.'

Niranjan Rajadhyaksha
Executive Director, Artha Global, and Former Executive Editor, Mint

'I found much to learn from this excellent basic economics primer

from Akash Kumar and Kumar Anand written in the tradition of Henry Hazlitt and Thomas Sowell.'
Katherine Mangu-Ward
Editor-in-Chief, Reason

'This book will make you smarter about India and smarter about economics. You will finish seeing prices, politicians and your local *mandi* differently. About as interesting as popular economics gets.'
Pieter Garicano
Managing Editor, Works in Progress

'I've built businesses for over three decades and picked up most of my economics through my entrepreneurial experience. I wish more of us thought clearly about how economies actually work. Kumar and Akash don't lecture; they make you see the world around us differently. A book about economics you actually can't put down; and the one India was missing. A must-read for everyone.'
Rajesh Jain
Serial Entrepreneur, Author and Founder, Netcore

'What is the magic that whisks mutton biryani to your doorstep within 15 minutes of dreaming of it? The answer is not "Zomato". Well, it may be, but that doesn't tell us how rice grown in Punjab, spices from Kerala, edible oil from Malaysia and a delivery boy from Jharkhand ring your doorbell at midnight. What are the forces that bring all these ingredients together to bring you a dish fit for kings? Who didn't have air-conditioning, by the way ... Economics is the study of satisfying our material desires, and in this delightful book, full of keen insight, Kumar and Akash tell us how economics works; and how, in the wrong hands, it is prevented from doing so.'
Mohit Satyanand
Entrepreneur and Investor

'I was delighted to read this book by Akash Kumar and Kumar Anand – it ended my search for a book that would help students and lay readers engage with critical topics in economics – money, price, profit, inflation; how citizens' life is affected through laws, rules, institutions, policies, incentives of public officials, suppliers, consumers and voters; how wealth is created – how citizens get to be wealthy and enjoy liberty; why some countries are poor and some are rich. And all of this written in a real-life and intimate style that holds readers' attention. I am sure this book will be immensely popular with teachers, students and other readers.'

Pankaj Das

Director, Modern English School, Kahilipara, Guwahati, Assam

'Kumar and Akash have done a great job to explain complex economics concepts in a way that non-economists can understand. This is a huge achievement. I hope that the ideas in this book on free markets, public choice, amongst others, get into mainstream debate so that India becomes a more prosperous country.'

Luis Miranda

Chairperson and Co-founder, Indian School of Public Policy, and Former Chairman, IDFC Private Equity

'Every Indian who reads a newspaper, argues about government spending and corruption, or wonders why the same government that sends a rocket to Mars cannot fix potholes – this book is for you. The authors give citizens the intellectual tools to ask the right questions and to resist the comfortable but seductive simplicity of bad ideas. What makes this book unique is how it teaches through stories that we all can easily recognize. By the time you reach the epilogue, you haven't just absorbed economic principles – you've seen them living inside the India you already know. As someone who has spent years championing the principles of market liberalism at the Centre for Civil Society, it is a proud moment to see these ideas find such vivid expression in Akash and Kumar's hands. This is nothing less than a masterful rendition of Bastiat's *Economic Sophisms* for an Indian audience!'

Parth J. Shah

Dean and Co-Founder, Indian School of Public Policy, and Founder, Centre for Civil Society

Quick and Concise

ECONOMICS

For Every Indian

Akash Kumar • Kumar Anand

hachette INDIA

First published in paperback in 2026 by Hachette India
(Registered name: Hachette Book Publishing India Pvt. Ltd)
An Hachette UK Company
www.hachetteindia.com

2

ISBN 978-93-5731-340-7

Hachette Book Publishing India Pvt. Ltd
4th & 5th Floors, Corporate Centre
Plot No. 94, Sector 44, Gurugram – 122003, India

Typeset in Athelas 10/13
by Avishek Bhattacharya

Printed and bound in India
by Manipal Technologies Limited

FSC www.fsc.org
MIX
Paper | Supporting responsible forestry
FSC™ C043100

For my father, Vijay Kumar Upadhyay – for engaging my curiosity early on; and my mother, Rekha Kumari – for turning scarce resources into abundant opportunity

– Akash

For my parents, Poonam Singh and Shyamanand Singh – the wisest and most optimistic people I know

– Kumar

IMAGE COPYRIGHT INFORMATION

1. Musical notes: Elionas/Pixabay
2. Quotation boxes: pikisuperstar/Freepik
3. Noteboxes: jensenartofficial/Pixabay
4. Page 1: Akbar: PD/ Metropolitan Museum of Art
5. Page2: Modern life: WHYFRAME/ Shutterstock
6. Page 4: X screenshot: PerBylund
7. Page 6: Ball smashing glass: JJ Jordan from Pexels
8. Page 9: Oval Maidan: Rakeshpate/CCA-SA 3.0 Unported licence
9. Page 12: Keynes: Unknown author/PD
10. Page 17: Oranges for sale: Sadat Ahmed/Pexels
11. Page 18: Adam Smith: Public domain
12. Page 19: Lithium mining: Freedom_wanted/ Shutterstock.com
13. Page 19: Phone assembly plant: PradeepGaurs/ Shutterstock.com
14. Page 21: Uninhabited island: Efraimstochter/ Pixabay
15. Page 21: Woman at supermarket: Tara Clark/ Pexels
16. Page 28: Donald Trump: Public domain/White House
17. Page 28: Henry George: Public domain
18. Page 30: A Tweet from @shruthibadri: shruthibadri
19. Page 35: Diet coke: Anna Holodna/Pexels
20. Page 36: Terminal 2, Kempegowda International Airport, Bengaluru: Ananthmohanram18/ CCA-SA 4.0 International licence
21. Page 37: Dhaba: PradeepGaurs/Shutterstock
22. Page 42: Kohli and Sharma: Bahnfrend/CCA-SA 4.0 International licence,
23. Page 43: Azadpur mandi by IFPRI South Asia, CC BY-NC-ND 2.0
24. Page 45: Demand-supply curve: Sanchit Khanna/Hindustan Times/Shutterstock
25. Page 51: Cold storage machinery: YASH DINESHBHAI PATEL/Shutterstock
26. Page 55: MGNREGA: Mulkh Singh/ CCA-SA 4.0 International licence
27. Page 60: 20-rupee coin: RBI/AstitvaGupta/ CCA-SA 4.0 International licence
28. Page 61: Man selling ice-cream: ParthaKar49/ Shutterstock
29. Page 62: Barter: illustrated by Avishek Bhattacharya ©Hachette India
30. Page 65: Bitcoin: IgorShubin/Pixabay
31. Page 66: Hundi: British government/Public domain
32. Page 66: Bank of Bengal: Bank of Bengal/Public domain
33. Page 68: An island: Fernando Reyes/ Pexels
34. Page 70: Covid 19: Anna Shvets/Pexels
35. Page 77: GDP: Jo Panuwat D/Shutterstock
36. Page 81: Cars: Ushindi Namegabe/Pexels
37. Page 82: Pani puri: Ganesh Dhamodkar/ Wikimedia Commons
38. Page 84: Burgers: Kezia Lynn/Pexels
39. Page 85: GDP per capita and HDI: Our World in Data
40. Page 86: Woman from Bhutan: Gaurav Bagdi/ Pexels
41. Page 90: Chinatown, Singapore: kallerna/CCA-SA 4.0 International licence
42. Page 91: Bangui: Z. Baddorf/VOA /Public domain
43. Page 93: Simon-Ehrlich Wager: Marian Tupy (https://humanprogress.org/wp-content/uploads/2025/01/01.jpg)
44. Page 95: Share of GDP: illustrated by Avishek Bhattacharya ©Hachette India
45. Page 98: Joel Mokyr: (המצולם) מוקיר יואל/CCA-SA 3.0 Unported licence (https://commons.wikimedia.org/wiki/File:Joel_Mokyr.png)
46. Page 102: Uber: Ilya Plekhanov/CCA-SA 4.0 International licence
47. Page 109: PCO: Flickr user banana chippy/ CCA-SA 3.0 Unported licence
48. Page 109: Mobile recharge shop: Dmitry Rukhlenko/Shutterstock
49. Page 111: Mobile phones have reached every corner: NIKS ADS/Shutterstock
50. Page 112: Cotton mill: Public domain/ Wikipedia
51. Page 118: Fixed pie fallacy: YesPhotographers/ Shutterstock
52. Page 121: Global Income Inequality: Marian Tupy
53. Page 126: Oxfam reports make headlines: illustrated by Avishek Bhattacharya ©Hachette India
54. Page 134: James Buccanan: Atlas Network
55. Page 134: Gordon Tullok: Joshua Paquin/ CCA-SA 3.0 Unported licence
56. Page 135: Voting: Hafiz Ahmed/ Shutterstock
57. Page 137: Netaji: neelstock/Shutterstock
58. Page 138: Aneesh ji: gfx_hamza/Shutterstock
59. Page 144: All illustrations: Sophia Ngayam ©Hachette India
60. Page 145: Police dumping alcohol: Unknown photographer, Orange County Archives/CCA 2.0 Generic licence
61. Page 146: Tata Truck: Proa 500/CCA-SA 4.0 International licence
62. Page 148: Painter: PRASANNAPIX/ Shutterstock
63. Page 154: Roman emperor: Dima Moroz/ Shutterstock
64. Page 155: Bands playing at a wedding: MARQUES P/Shutterstock
65. Page 155: A wedding ritual: Ritesh Ranjan Sett/ Shutterstock
66. Page 155: Food at a wedding: Putu Esa/ Shutterstock
67. Page 160: Ashok Hotel: dasari002/Shutterstock
68. Page 160: Condoms: SAM THOMAS A/ Shutterstock
69. Page 160: BSNL: sdx15/Shutterstock
70. Page 162: Gurugram: ANUJA SHARMA/ Shutterstock
71. Page 164: Dorabji Tata Park: Arnav Pratap Singh/Shutterstock
73. Page 166: Stubble burning: Aamir Mushtaq91/ Shutterstock
74. Page 167: Monopoly: illustrated by Avishek Bhattacharya ©Hachette India
75. Page 169: Coal mining: creativevikas/ Shutterstock
76. Page 169: Maruti Swift: Salilz/Shutterstock
77. Page 172: Medical diagnosis: Ground Picture/ Shutterstock

CONTENTS

I

WHAT IS ECONOMICS REALLY?

The Seen and the Unseen

♪ *Aankhen khuli ho ya ho band, deedar unka hota hai* ♪

FROM SCARCITY TO ABUNDANCE – HOW?

Figure 1.1: Akbar

It is May 1580 – a scorching hot afternoon. Emperor Akbar sits in his Agra palace, servants fanning him with peacock feathers that fail to do much against the heat. Lunch is here – the usual 40 dishes, impressive to count, boring to eat. Same recipes his grandfather knew. The tomatoes that would go on to transform the Mughlai cuisine as we know it today are still sailing somewhere in the Portuguese ships. What about the potatoes that would go in the *aloo gosht*? Or the chilies that would make curry? All these ingredients are still waiting their turn in history.

When his tooth throbs with pain that evening, the *Shahenshah-e-Hind* has three choices: suffer in imperial silence, chew cloves just like a commoner does, or let the royal *hakim* yank it out with pliers while he lets out a scream trying to bite down on leather. The Mughals could conquer kingdoms but couldn't conquer a cavity. No anaesthesia, no antibiotics, just pain and plain old prayers (or the new *Deen-i-ilahi* ones, who knows?).

Entertainment? Akbar claps his hands. Musicians arrive ... eventually. The same musicians he had heard yesterday. And the day before. Well, now he wants to hear a different style. Maybe something from the Carnatic tradition? Too bad. Those musicians are a three-month journey away.

Akbar wants to send an urgent message to Birbal who is touring Bengal. The fastest horse relay will take two weeks. Each way. By the time he gets a reply, the urgent issue might have become a crisis. Or resolved itself. He has no way of even knowing.

Figure 1.2: Modern life

Now picture yourself, dear reader. You're lying in bed with that AC at a perfect 24°C, debating whether to order pizza, Thai curry or a healthy protein bowl. You take out Toblerone chocolate from your fridge. It has travelled all the way from Switzerland and still tastes yummy. Feeling a little bit under the weather? You turn up the AC temperature just a little bit, pop that Dolo 650 from your cabinet and get under your breathable microfibre blanket. You are shuffling songs on Spotify and going from Arijit Singh to A.R. Rahman and from Beethoven to K-pop, all in no time. All this while you are chatting on WhatsApp with your best friend from college. Who's really living like royalty?

What is the source of this abundance? How did all this come about? How is it that such comforts have become available to most people in just a span of a few centuries? All this while the world's population has seen a 16x increase – up from approximately 500 million in the sixteenth century to over eight billion today. Of course, this by no means is to say that our world is perfect at this time. But it is also true that the general trend of progress over the last many centuries has been upwards and it looks promising for the future as well.[1]

As lifelong students of economics ourselves, this question has fascinated us no end: How is it that in a world of finite and depleting resources and growing population, we have a continuously improving well-being for the masses, increasing prosperity, increasing life expectancy and so on? There are many chapters in the book that attempt to answer this very question as there are many layers to how this abundance came to be.

Chapter 1 gives you a brief snapshot on how this relative prosperity is an anomaly in the millennia-old world history. Chapter 5 deals with why we see this much more in some countries than others. Chapter 6 deals with how the sudden spurt of innovation unleashed this prosperity.

WHAT IS ECONOMICS ABOUT?

Per Bylund
@PerBylund

What causes #poverty? Nothing. It's the original state, the default and starting point. The real question is, What causes #prosperity?

2:34 PM · 15 Nov 2015

461 12.8K

Figure 1.3: A Tweet from @PerBylund[2]

Economics is about making choices.

People make choices all the time. You deciding to pick up this book is a choice. At this moment, you are choosing to read these lines, at the cost of all other things you could be doing with your time and money.

People are economizing beings. We try to do more with less. Our world is that of limited means and unlimited wants, that of limited resources and unlimited needs. We live in a world of finite resources and a growing population. Our world also has continuously improving well-being, growing prosperity, improving health and life expectancy. How could it be? How could finite resources and a growing population still lead to better quality of life and improved well-being? In essence, economics studies all that entails this economizing process.

Wealth is not necessarily more money. Wealth is more goods and services for people to consume. Therefore, in so far as more money represents access to more goods and services, by possessing more money, one can be called wealthy. To create more money without creating more goods and services is not to create more wealth but only more inflation. *(Connect the dots: Turn to page 69.)*

So the bad news is that we cannot print our way to prosperity. The good news is that we have steadily moved from scarcity towards abundance. This is not an accident.

Most of the world was poor and had terrible living conditions till, say, 1800. What happened then that changed the course of our human civilization in ways depicted in the graph below? We will talk about it more in the chapters to come. *(Connect the dots: Turn to pages 112–113.)*

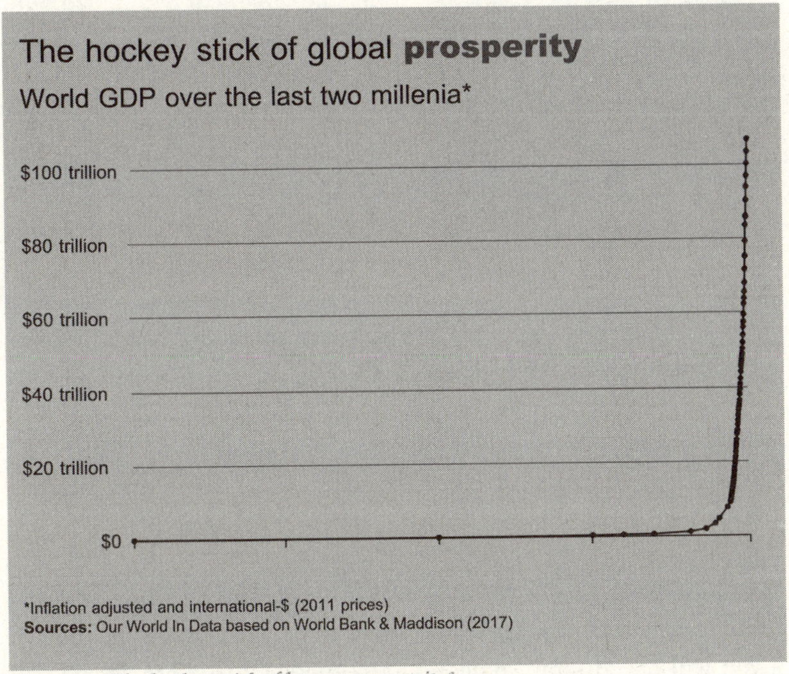

Figure 1.4: The hockey stick of human prosperity[3]

CRICKET BALL AND ECONOMICS IN ONE LESSON

The summer afternoon buzzed with energy as 12-year-old Akash and his friends gathered for their daily cricket match. The sun hung high in the sky, casting short shadows on the makeshift cricket pitch they had created using spare bricks as wickets.

Akash was batting, feeling particularly confident after scoring well in the previous over. As the bowler ran up, he gripped his bat tighter,

Figure 1.5: Cricket ball and Economics in One Lesson

eyes on the approaching ball. With a powerful swing, he connected perfectly – perhaps too perfectly. The ball soared high into the air, sailing over the boundary and straight towards Aniket's house.

C-R-A-S-H!

The sound of breaking glass brought their game to an abrupt halt. The children stood frozen, watching as Aniket rushed to his window, his face red in anger. The window had a perfect cricket ball-sized hole in it, with cracks spreading like a spider's web across the remaining glass.

'Sorry, uncle!' Akash called out, his voice trembling slightly. As the children waited with bated breath to head home and face the consequences, Akash's friend Surlay tried to cheer him up.

'You know what, uncle?' he told Aniket, putting an arm around Akash's shoulders. 'Maybe this isn't such a bad thing after all. Think about it – you will have to hire someone to fix the window. That person will earn money, and then they'll probably spend it at other shops in our neighborhood. It's like you're helping the local economy!'

Wasn't he right, after all? It might be a net loss for Aniket, but isn't it a net gain for society?

No, it's not. It is a classic economic fallacy, first highlighted by Frederic Bastiat. It's called the broken window theory, surely after the incident Akash got into!

Here's where the fallacy kicks in: This thinking ignores what Aniket would have done with that money if he hadn't needed to fix the window. Perhaps he was saving to buy his children a present or planning to invest in his *kirana* shop or even looking to treat his family to a nice dinner. When the window breaks, Aniket is forced to spend money on returning to the status quo before – simply getting back what he already had, a functional window. He doesn't gain anything new. The money that goes to the glazier would have gone to the gift shop or the restaurant or in Aniket's own business, potentially creating much more value rather than just replacing something that was destroyed.

Surlay, and for that matter most people, are only seeing what is immediately visible. They'll see the broken glass and the fixed glass but would never see the gifts or that dinner that could've been, precisely because it'll not materialize now.

Just think of it this way: If breaking windows really helped the economy, we could make everyone prosperous by going around breaking all the windows in town! We can see how that wouldn't make any sense. Destruction never creates real prosperity. Real growth comes from creation and innovation, not from having to replace things that were broken.[4]

What are the broken windows in government policy around us today? Think about it.

One of the most famous introductory economics books of the twentieth century was Henry Hazlitt's *Economics in One Lesson*. In the book he was channeling the key lesson from Frederic Bastiat, famous French economist of the nineteenth century. According to Hazlitt, economics can be summarized in one lesson:

> The art of economics consists in looking not merely at the immediate but at the **longer effects of any act or policy**; it consists in tracing the consequences of that policy not merely for one group but **for all groups**.
>
> – **Henry Hazlitt**, *Economics in One Lesson*[5] (1946)

An understanding of economics is crucial for everyone interested in how things work in a society, what keeps the modern world going, and our individual place in it.

TWO KINDS OF ORDER IN SOCIETY: SPONTANEOUS ORDER AND PLANNED ORDER

Open spaces are in short supply. Nowhere more so than in Mumbai.

Across from the famous Churchgate station in south Mumbai is Oval Maidan. You pass through the Oval on a weekday and the *maidan* will mostly be empty, except for the people crossing through the ground to get to their office in Fort or to visit Gateway of India or the flea market on Colaba causeway.

However, on a weekend, the story is not the same. On Saturdays, Sundays and holidays, the ground is filled with people and activity. A single contiguous piece of land that is 25 acres in area has 22 pitches, and 44 teams playing on any given day. Hundreds of people can be seen playing cricket with overlapping pitches and fielding areas.

For an outsider passing by, this may look chaotic. However, upon closer examination, one can see that there is an order in the chaos. People are not fighting to control scarce resources, in this case, a public ground for them to play cricket. Rather, they seem to get along and share the

Figure 1.6: Oval Maidan in Mumbai

ground in a manner that makes for a more efficient use, probably the most efficient use under the circumstance.

One can find such order – known as 'spontaneous order' – in the seeming chaos all around us. Spontaneous orders are easy to miss, as we take them for granted. Our mind and eyes are trained (have evolved) to appreciate and marvel at orders that are more symmetrical and planned.

Contrast the weekend Oval *maidan* activity with an Indian Premier League (IPL) cricket match in Wankhede Stadium where only two teams are playing, and at no time more than 15 people are on the ground when a match is on – 11 players from the bowling side, two batsmen, and two umpires. From the outside, it can seem as the contrasting stories of chaos versus order. But essentially, they are just two kinds of orders. The only difference is that one is a planned order and the other a spontaneous order.

If we pause and observe, we can see these two different kinds of order all around us.

There are some essential features of these two different kinds of order. One has a centralized top-down plan, while the other one has individuals making their own plans. In one, the outcomes can be forecast ahead of time, in the other, they cannot.

Every six months or so, when you walk into your neighbourhood mall, you will see that some shops have closed down and new ones have opened up in their place. None of this could be forecast ahead of time. It is a result of hundreds and thousands of people making individual choices to buy or not to buy from a shop – the more a shop does business, it thrives and grows and the less a shop does business, it is forced to shut down. Whether a business thrives or closes depends on how well they are able to serve their customers, compared to choices available.

Some of the classic examples of spontaneous order are language, money, law, cities and markets.

No one person came up with the language that we speak today, just as no single person came up with the money we use, or the laws that govern us and customs that we follow. These are all results of millions of people interacting over a long period of time and not limited to an individual mind or time period. These outcomes have not been shaped by deliberate human design, but have resulted from unplanned cooperation among lots of people over a long period of time, in some cases stretching over centuries and millennia.

These are also orders that are constantly evolving. New words keep getting added to the language we speak, money we use is constantly evolving in its nature and the laws and customs change with time as well.

Spontaneous orders are robust. And robust orders are often spontaneous.[6]

What other examples of spontaneous orders can you spot from your life?

WHY THIS BOOK? WHO IS THIS BOOK FOR?

Highlighting the immense dynamism and complexity of our modern world, British economist Tim Harford noted in his 2017 book:[7]

> The world economy defies comprehension. A continuously changing system of immense complexity, it offers **over ten billion distinct products and services**, doubles in size every fifteen years and links almost every one of the planet's **seven billion people**. It delivers astonishing luxury to hundreds of millions. It also leaves hundreds of millions behind, puts tremendous strains on the ecosystem and has an alarming habit of stalling. Nobody is in charge of it. Indeed, no individual understands more than a fraction of what's going on.

Indeed, our modern world is complex and constantly changing. Making sense of this rapidly changing world can be a daunting task. Of all the social sciences, we think economics is best placed to help understand our world.

Every citizen of India is a stakeholder in the well-being of the nation. Some of us may choose to ignore economics and policy ideas that determine our fortunes, but ideas – good and bad – affect *all* of us. The way our political system is designed – laws, rules and institutions that govern us – determines the quality of our life.

Ideas and institutions that govern India are different compared with other countries, at times appearing less than the best but certainly not the worst. The objective of this book is to introduce readers to ideas that have the potential to transform our institutions and have far-reaching consequences for our well-being. This book also diagnoses our current state of affairs and builds an understanding of what is working, and where all and how we can do better.

The power of ideas is often understated and underappreciated. Economist John Maynard Keynes famously said:[8]

> The ideas of economists and political philosophers, both when they are right and when they are wrong, are more powerful than is commonly understood. Indeed, the world is ruled by little else. Practical men, who believe themselves to be quite exempt from any intellectual influences, are usually slaves of some defunct economist.

Ideas have consequences. Ideas are powerful. Good ideas can change lives and transform nations, just as bad ideas can destroy them. This book also puts together great ideas that have stood the test of time and helped societies prosper. We hope the lessons contained in this book will open a new way of policy thinking for you, as these once did for us.

Figure 1.7: John Maynard Keynes

These ideas have been shared with readers with only common sense as our tool and little or no technical knowledge previously required. All the lessons will be shared in a manner that is easily relatable with day-to-day economic and policy affairs.

A typical economics textbook may require a lot from an average person in order to follow and absorb all the lessons. After all, the textbook is expressly written for those on their path to become professional economists. This book is an attempt to make economics accessible to everyone. If you persist with us, we promise that by the end, you will have answers to many of the everyday phenomena you've always wondered about.

KEY TAKEAWAYS

- What causes **poverty**? Nothing. It's the original state, the default and starting point. The real question is, what causes **prosperity**? Economic history of the world is that of movement **from scarcity to abundance through exchange and that movement is a much more recent phenomenon than we think it is.**
- **Economics is about choices.** We always give up something to get something else.
- **We can't print our way to prosperity.** Money without production causes inflation.
- **Real wealth is not money but access to goods and services.**
- Destruction never creates real prosperity.
- Ideas have consequences.

- A good economist looks not **merely at the immediate** but at the **long-term effects** of any act or policy; and traces the consequences of that policy **not merely for one group** but **for all groups.**

2

Why Doing Everything by Yourself Is a Terrible Idea?

Exchange, Specialization and Trade

♪ Ek aur ek gyarah, mere yaara ♪

Do you know how many people it takes to make a pencil and what master plan they use to coordinate?[1] The answer lies in something you witness every day but probably never notice. Or for that matter your morning cup of coffee at Blue Tokai? You're holding that cup of coffee. You saw the barista ground the beans, boil the water and pour it through a V60 filter. But by himself he did not make that cup of coffee. Rather, he can't.

Neither can you. Neither can anyone on earth. Not a single human being alive possesses the full range of knowledge, skill and labour required to produce a single cup of coffee from scratch. Johan Norberg in his book *The Capitalist Manifesto*[2] recounts the story of A.J. Jacobs, a journalist who decided to test this idea in the most literal way possible. He wanted to personally thank every single person involved in producing his morning cup of coffee. He started at his local café in New York. He thought it might involve a few dozen people.

It involved over a thousand. The barista. The bean buyer. The roaster. The trucker. The warehouse pest-control specialist. The woman who tested the water from the watershed. The Colombian farming family who rose before dawn. The Minnesota miners who extracted the iron that became the steel in his coffee roaster. The pallet-makers. The lid designer. Someone had to design the lid, and it turns out the engineering of a coffee cup lid is a small miracle of fluid dynamics and ergonomics that most of us have never paused to consider. His cup of coffee, he discovered, started nine months before he drank it and travelled over four thousand kilometres on motorcycles, trucks and ships before reaching his hands.[3]

DOUBLE THANK-YOU MOMENTS

Watch any transaction at a street-side *thela*. The uncle haggling over oranges finally agrees to ₹50 per kilogram. As he pays, both he and the vendor often say '*theek hai*' or even 'thank you'. Why? Because despite all the bargaining drama, both got something they wanted more than what they gave up. The vendor wanted the ₹50 more than his oranges. The uncle wanted the oranges more than his ₹50. The very fact that the uncle chose to part with his hard-earned money for the street vendor's fruit and the street vendor chose to take the money in exchange is proof that both parties walk away from the exchange better off than before. Both won. That's the magic of trade.

The key feature behind every voluntary exchange is that it makes both the buyer and the seller better off. If the exchange were to make either of them worse off, the exchange would not take place.

These are all occasions of what journalist Josh Stossel calls double

Figure 2.1: Oranges for sale

thank-you moments.[4] That is, occasions where both parties of exchange say 'thank you' to the other as they walk away. They may not have got the deal they wanted but were certainly willing to exchange at the agreed upon rate or price. It is important to note here that each act of exchange makes both the parties better off. *(Connect the dots: Turn to page 38.)*

Trade and voluntary exchange, in other words 'double thank-you moments', are the source of all our achievements. Higher the number of double thank-you moments, the more prosperous an individual is. As it essentially means more occasions to benefit through trade and exchange, there are more occasions to make a profit. The same is true for a business and for the country.

That human beings exchange voluntarily with one another is what sets us apart from all other mammals. Trade is how something can come out of nothing. Trade is how individuals, businesses and nations without any initial endowment can go on to become infinitely prosperous.

Someone may think that you need to be born into a rich family to live a life of abundance. That a country needs to be rich with natural resources for it to become a developed country. That someone will be wrong in assuming this. *(Connect the dots: Turn to pages 92–93.)*

Congo in Africa is well endowed with natural resources, but it is also one of the poorest countries in the world. Hong Kong and Singapore are among the richest jurisdictions without much natural resources within their geographical boundaries. Steve Jobs, one of the most accomplished individuals in recent history, was not born into a rich family, and in fact dropped out of college to avoid spending his adoptive parents' savings on tuition.

The world is full of examples where individuals, businesses and nation states began with nothing and went on to create unimaginable wealth and prosperity for themselves.

This week try to notice every 'double thank-you moment' in your life. From your morning *chai* to your evening auto ride. You're part of an incredible web of voluntary exchange that would make Adam Smith smile.

HOW DOES YOUR MOBILE PHONE GET TO YOU?

Figure 2.2: Adam Smith

Adam Smith (1723–90) was a Scottish economist and philosopher. He is also known as the father of economics for his seminal book *An Inquiry into the Nature and Causes of the Wealth of Nations* (1776). Smith argued that the main cause of prosperity was increasing division of labour.[5] Let's see that with a modern example.

That phone in your pocket is a miracle and I'm not even talking about the technology. The technology certainly is impressive, but what is more impressive is how many millions of people coordinated for you to be able to get that phone.

Figure 2.3: Lithium mining

Let me break down what had to happen for that ₹15,000 Samsung device to reach your local mobile shop.

Lithium miners in the Atacama Desert of Chile wake up at 5 a.m. to extract metal they'll never see turned into batteries. They don't know you exist.

They definitely don't know you were comparing phones at Vijay Sales last Sunday. Yet somehow, they mined exactly enough lithium to ensure your phone was in stock.

Meanwhile, an engineer at the Taiwan Semiconductor Manufacturing Company (TSMC) fabricated the chips on machines that cost more than private jets. She doesn't know if you prefer Samsung, Xiaomi or Apple. She can't predict whether Indians will buy 200 million or 300 million phones this year. Yet somehow, the right chips were ready at the right time.

In a factory in Noida, workers assembled these parts – Chilean lithium, Taiwanese chips, Korean displays, and Chinese cameras – into the phone you're holding. The factory manager has never met the Chilean miners or Taiwanese engineers. He definitely hasn't met you. Yet everyone's efforts synchronized

Figure 2.4: Phone assembly plant in Noida

perfectly to put that phone in your hands.

Could anyone or even ten workers – no matter how smart or hard-working – have produced this phone all by themselves?

SOURCE OF ALL OUR PROSPERITY IS TRADE

If each of us were to make all the things we need on a daily basis, we would all be poor and would not have access to all the goods and services that we have come to take for granted today. It is 'division of labour' and 'specialization' in practice where each of us do a few things that we are good at, exchange our services for money, and use that money to buy all that we need.

According to Adam Smith, circumstances leading up to abundance through specialization are dexterity, saving time in switching tasks and innovation.

If we do the same thing again and again, we become more efficient at it; we become dextrous. Also, if we don't have to do all the tasks involved in, say making a pin, then we don't lose time in switching between tasks. And as we continue to do the same task, over a period of time, human ingenuity and our urge to do the task quickly and with less effort spurs innovation. These are the building blocks underlying our modern world that becomes more abundant each day.

Is there a limit to division of labour and in turn to specialization, and thereby, to our prosperity? Yes, there is. That's the bad news. The good news is that this limit is of our own making and we can also get rid of it easily.

Imagine if you were alone on an uninhabited island. You would have no occasion to exchange, as you have no one to exchange with. You

Figure 2.5: An uninhabited island

will need to take care of food, water, shelter and so on, on your own. You alone will have to gather coconuts or fish for food, make fire to prepare that food, gather drinking water in coconut shells for when you are thirsty and find a place to sleep away from rain, wind and maybe wild animals. Sounds dreadful!

Now if another person were to arrive on the island, you have an occasion to celebrate as it is in both your interest to cooperate by dividing the tasks among yourselves that each of you are good at and exchanging at the end of the day. The total amount of goods produced in such a scenario when there is cooperation and each of you are specializing will be way more than when each of you was not cooperating and making things only for yourself.

Now imagine there are a hundred people in a village cooperating and trading among themselves. What about a small town of a few thousand people? A metro city of a few millions? A state with a population of tens of millions? The entire country of over 1.4 billion people! The entire world of over eight billion people!

Figure 2.6: Trade brings abundance

It is our tendency to trade that allows us to specialize by practising division of labour. As the number of people we can potentially trade with increases, division of labour will be higher and higher will be the level of specialization. That's the interconnected world we live in today – where we buy and sell goods and services from people all over the world.

> As it is the power of exchanging that gives occasion to the division of labour, so the extent of this division must always be limited by the extent of that power, or, in other words, by the extent of the market.
>
> – **Adam Smith**, *The Wealth of Nations* (1776)[5]

So what limits division of labour? Division of labour is limited by the extent of the market.

But will this system benefit all? What about those who are not born into connections and money or are otherwise not too smart and entrepreneurial?

For trade to take place, both buyer and seller should have what the other person wants, which leaves both parties better off after the exchange. What about those who have little to no initial endowment? What about those who are slow compared with others? Does trade leave them behind?

COMPARATIVE ADVANTAGE

The concept of comparative advantage is one of the most powerful and also one of the most counter-intuitive concepts in economics. It was developed over two hundred years ago by economist David Ricardo.[6]

Let's understand this concept through a puzzle.

More Cricket, Less Chores – a Challenge

Adithya and Prashanth are teenage twins who live with their parents in Bengaluru. Every Sunday evening, they have to do household chores – laundry and dishes – and that too when IPL matches are telecast on TV.

Here's the thing: Adithya is simply faster at everything. He can finish ironing his shirts in 30 minutes and washing his dishes in 60 minutes. The younger Prashanth takes 120 minutes to do the ironing and 90 minutes to do the dishes. Same results, just slower hands.

	Adithya	Prashanth
Ironing clothes	30 minutes	120 minutes
Doing dishes	60 minutes	90 minute

Both brothers desperately want to finish their chores and catch the game because their team Royal Challengers Bengaluru is going head-to-head with the favourites Chennai Super Kings. None of them wants to miss seeing Virat Kohli bat. Prashanth has a lightbulb moment. 'Bro,' he says to Adithya, 'what if we trade our chores?'

Adithya laughs. 'Maga, I'm faster at everything. How would this help?'

Pause and think: Before reading on, can you solve their puzzle? How can both brothers save time?

Solution to 'More Cricket, Less Chores – a Challenge'

Clearly, Adithya is faster at doing both laundry and dishes. In other words, Adithya has an *absolute advantage* in doing both laundry and dishes.

But Prashanth had noticed something clever. While Adithya is faster at both tasks, he's *especially* fast at ironing the shirts – he can iron his shirts in just 30 minutes, which is one-fourth the time Prashanth takes. But for dishes, Adithya takes 60 minutes compared with Prashanth's 90 minutes.

So it may appear that there is no way Prashanth can offer a deal to Adithya that benefits both siblings – that is, it saves both of them time doing chores and thus allows them to start watching the Sunday evening cricket match earlier.

The brilliant idea that Prashanth has to trade chores in a manner that benefits both siblings makes use of the fact that while Adithya has an absolute advantage in doing both ironing shirts and doing the dishes, he has a *comparative advantage* in doing dishes.

Here's Prashanth's proposal to Adithya:
Brother, granted you are better than me at doing both ironing the clothes and doing the dishes. But if you only iron both our clothes, it will take you a total of 30 + 30 minutes, which is an hour. That's half an hour less than what it would have taken for you to iron your clothes and do your dishes (30 + 60 minutes).

I'll wash our plates. Doing all the dishes will take me 90 + 90 minutes which is three hours. But that's still half an hour less than what it'd have taken me to iron my clothes and do my dishes.

Both of us save half an hour each and if I start early, I might also be able to see Kohli bat. You definitely will.

Here's the tabular representation of this trade:

	Adithya (time in minutes)	Prashanth (time in minutes)
Adithya's clothes	30	-
Adithya's dishes	-	90
Prashanth's clothes	30	-
Prashanth's dishes	-	90
Total	60	180
Total (before the swapping of chores)	90	210
Difference (time saved)	30	30

You don't need to be the best at something to have a comparative advantage. Even the person who is 'slower' or 'less productive' at every task has something valuable to trade. It is this brilliant idea that allows individuals and corporations around the world to trade with each other even when one particular individual or corporation is more efficient than their trading partner at doing all things.

A person has a comparative advantage at producing something if that person can produce it at a lower cost than anyone else. It is important to note here that to have a comparative advantage in a good or service does not mean one is the absolute best at producing it. Someone can be completely lacking in skills at doing something and yet have a comparative advantage at doing it! Just as Prashanth is less skilled than

Adithya at both ironing and doing dishes, but he has a comparative advantage at doing dishes, as he is the least-cost producer for the latter.

This goes for even Adithya's and Prashanth's favourite cricketer. Most likely, Virat Kohli doesn't mow his own lawn even though he could probably do it faster than his gardener who's not as fit as Kohli is. But Kohli's time is better spent practising cricket, where his advantage is massive. The gardener, meanwhile, specializes in lawn care. Both are better off when they trade.

This is one of the most important lessons in economics, summarized in one sentence: *Do what you do best, and trade for the rest.* But if trade is so good, why do we not trade as much as we can?

TARIFFS AND PROTECTIONISM

The Great Indian Shortage Age

It's 1980. Your father has finally saved enough to buy a car. He walks into the showroom with cash in hand, ready to drive home his dream vehicle. His choices? A Premier Padmini or an Ambassador. Both cars were designed when Nehru *ji* was still alive, and were essentially museum pieces on wheels, guzzled petrol like thirsty camels and cost more than many people's houses.

The salesman smiles apologetically: 'Sir, please fill this form. The waiting period is currently ... errr seven years.'

Seven years.[7]

Your mother's arthritis will worsen over those seven years, but she'll keep taking the overcrowded Delhi Transport Corporation (DTC) bus to work, standing even when her knees are protesting because seats are easily taken up by the young passengers who are more agile. Your father will retire before the car arrives; that dream of a family road trip to Shimla will be forever postponed.

This wasn't Soviet Russia. This was India, where buying a car meant putting your life on hold.

Why this *Kolaveri*? Licences. Permits. Quotas.

The government determined how much the automobile industry should be allowed to produce. It had also built walls – massive import duties of 200 per cent, sometimes 300 per cent – to 'protect' our car industry. The logic went: Keep foreign cars out, and Indian companies will flourish. Indian jobs will be saved. We'll become self-reliant – *Aatmanirbhar* – before it was cool (it never is).

What actually happened? Protection and coddling resulted in complacency. Why innovate when customers have no choice? Fuel efficiency and cost optimization that could have evolved in the industry's advancement did not happen as anticipated. A predictable retort would be allowing imported cars would destroy our jobs. But that's a fallacy. The lump of labour fallacy in that retort assumes that there is only a finite, fixed amount of work in the economy to go around. This is not true. The nature of work is not static and is constantly evolving, but we are wired to think in a zero-sum way.

Lower prices induce more demand, which might make the domestic automobile industry more competitive and it might even generate a lot more jobs as more competitive domestic manufacturers find a larger domestic market and even new markets abroad as a result of innovation and economies of scale. Even in the worst case where manufacturers are unable to cope with competition, it simply means jobs move to new industries. *(Connect the dots: Turn to page 110.)*

Who Really Pays for Protection?

Tariffs are back in the news, thanks to President Trump. Hopefully by the time this book reaches you, the world would have already seen the disastrous results of those policies, and countries would have reversed course.

Figure 2.7: Donald Trump

So while President Trump might be proclaiming tariffs as a punishment on countries he doesn't like in that moment, they are actually a tax on his own citizens as much as they are a bother to companies in the foreign countries he is targeting. When his government puts a 50 per cent tariff on imported goods from a certain country, who is paying? It's added to the price in due time and the consumers pay for it.

Figure 2.8: Henry George

> *What protection teaches us is to do to ourselves in time of peace what enemies seek to do to us in time of war.*
>
> – **Henry George**, *Protection or Free Trade (1886)*[8]

But ... Who Benefits?

Why is protectionism so popular then? When a textile mill in Surat has to shut down because it can't compete with Chinese imports, the five hundred lost jobs have names and faces. They show up on the news.

The mill owner meets the local MLA. The workers protest at Jantar Mantar. The pain is visible. It is concentrated, and politically potent. But the 50 crore Indians who save ₹100 each on clothing every year because of those same imports? That's ₹5,000 crore in savings – a hundred times more than those workers' annual wages. But those savings are invisible, spread thin across a billion purchases. No one marches in the streets to thank China for cheaper school uniforms. No mother writes to her MP saying 'Thanks to imports, I could afford two sets of clothes for my children this Diwali instead of one.' *(Connect the dots: Turn to pages 140–142.)*

In the short to medium term, protectionism benefits a few traders who are shielded from foreign competition as they enjoy a captive domestic market whose consumers don't have a choice but to buy from them. In the long term, these protected producers also lose as they stand no chance against the constant improvement in productivity of foreign producers, whenever the trade barriers are lifted. *(Connect the dots: Turn to pages 30 and 104.)*

> *An infant industry, if coddled, tends to remain an infant industry and never grows up or expands.*
>
> **– John James Cowperthwaite**[9]

A Tariff on Import Is Often Also a Tariff on Export

Rajesh Anna runs a small garment export business in Tiruppur. Last year, he lost a massive Lululemon contract to a factory in Bangladesh. 'Their quote was 15 per cent lower,' he told me, frustrated. 'I can't match it even with zero profit.'

How? Indian workers aren't being paid significantly higher than Bangladeshi workers. Neither are the factories in Bangladesh

Shruthi Badri
@shruthibadri

was looking into why my favorite clothing brands manufactured in pakistan, china, turkey but not india...and the answer was not labour or skills, but technical fabric!

this modern fabric is subject to a gst structure where the raw material faces higher taxes (18%) than the finished product (5%)

combined with other barriers like anti-dumping duties and other tariffs makes raw material 30% more expensive in india!

8:00 PM · May 9, 2025

10 Retweets 26 Quote Tweets 277 Likes

Figure 2.9: A Tweet from @shruthibadri[10]

more advanced. There isn't much of a skill or productivity gap either. How are they still able to consistently undercut Indian manufacturers? The answer is in a roll of synthetic fabric. That moisture-wicking material in your gym clothes. The quick-dry fabric in swimwear. The stretchy fabric in sleek, curve-hugging bodycon dresses. All of that is imported synthetic fabric – polyester, nylon, spandex blends. It's a story of how India shoots itself in the foot with tariffs.

By the time Rajesh Anna imports this fabric, government fees would have made it over ~25 per cent more expensive than what his Bangladeshi competitors pay (take 20 per cent import tariffs + Goods and Services Tax (GST) + surcharges). Garment manufacturing is a brutal, thin-margin business and something like this just delivers a fatal blow to our own manufacturers. (Some of the GST structures have undergone reform since September 2025.[11])

What's the result? Nike, Zara, Uniqlo. They are sourcing from Vietnam, Turkey, Bangladesh and even Pakistan. Not because they don't like India but because our tariff structure makes us uncompetitive in the kind of clothes where global demand is exploding.

Each of the garment factories in India employs hundreds of people, mostly women. Tiruppur alone could add lakhs of new jobs if it was allowed to compete in synthetic garments. But our counterproductive tariff policy ensures those jobs end up going to women in Dhaka, and not Dharapuram.

So, why did the government follow this policy? The government imposed these tariffs to 'protect' the domestic polyester manufacturers. How many people do the polyester industry employ? Four to five million by any measure. While the ready-made garments sector directly employs 12 to 13 million with the potential to double that number if the industry becomes export competitive. In trying to become self-reliant in everything, we've made ourselves uncompetitive in areas where we had the natural edge. We could have dominated in these sectors globally, but we made a conscious policy choice otherwise.

Despite all geopolitical uncertainties of recent times, the most extensive and robust supply chains are the ones that are spread across the world. Every time we tariff those inputs to protect our domestic producers, we are handicapping our 'could have been' exports. It does not end with polyester – steel tariffs are hurting engineering exports, chemical tariffs are hurting pharma exports and component tariffs are hurting electronics assembly.

Rajesh Anna still runs his factory, now focused on cotton basics where India remains somewhat competitive. But every time he sees a moisture-wicking athletic wear at Nike, he thinks of the contracts that could have been his – if only we understood that *a tariff on imports is really a tariff on our own exports.*

THE BOTTOM LINE

Tariffs limit the extent of the market by creating barriers to trade.

A limited extent of the market thus limits division of labour and specialization, which in turn leads to lower productivity. Tariffs and other trade restrictions thus add to scarcity and draws from abundance.

Since World War II, average tariffs around the world have been declining. But recent global events have been a cause for worry.

Trade is almost always a friendly exchange when conducted voluntarily. Indeed, they are double thank-you moments. Imposition of tariffs on the other hand is considered a hostile act. Protection, sanction and embargo suggest hostility.

It is therefore for the general peace and prosperity of all who inhabit this world that we move away from a more-protectionist to a less-protectionist world.

Every time someone says we need to protect an industry, ask:

- Protect from what? Better products? Lower prices? Innovation?
- Protect for whom? The few producers or crores of consumers?
- Protect until when? Another decade? Another century?

Pause and think: What products do you use daily that wouldn't exist if India had protected itself from foreign goods?

KEY TAKEAWAYS

- **Voluntary exchange benefits both parties,** creating double thank-you moments.

- **Division of labour increases productivity**, letting people focus on what they do best.
- **Specialization leads to efficiency**, saving time and boosting innovation.
- **The more people you can trade with, the larger the size of the market and the richer people get** – prosperity grows with market size.
- **Doing everything by yourself is a sure-shot way to poverty** – cooperation makes all of us better off. The key lesson is **Do what you do best, trade for the rest.**
- **Even 'laggards' win in a trade** – the person worst at everything still benefits through comparative advantage (counter-intuitive, yet very crucial).
- **Tariffs and protectionism hurt consumers** by limiting choice and raising prices. These might help a few businesses but hurt millions of consumers and eventually workers as well.
- **Competition increases the total number of jobs, even if it destroys some of them.**
- **Free trade expands markets**, promotes peace, and drives long-term economic growth.
- **Trade is the engine of prosperity** – it is what turns scarcity into abundance.
- **Abundance doesn't need riches or resources** – it needs exchange, openness and ideas.

3

WHAT ARE PRICES TRYING TO TELL YOU?

Prices as Signals

♪Suno na, suno na, sun lo na♪

Have you ever spent an entire Sunday cooking an elaborate meal only to have your family eat it half-heartedly while eyeing the samosas your uncle brought? You invested time, money and effort thinking these automatically create value. We like to think value is something solid, measurable, sitting inside objects like stuffing inside a samosa – this amount of labour corresponds to this amount of value. But that's completely backwards.

This little secret that you've just learned is so simple and yet so counter-intuitive that for over a century, brilliant minds – from Adam Smith and David Ricardo to Karl Marx – all expressed their concepts of value backwards. They believed value lay in labour and value for any object was determined by the amount of 'socially necessary' labour required to produce it.[1] But ***value comes from what others get out of it, not what you put in.***

Yet there're those who keep forgetting this lesson even today, particularly governments. They'll spend crores building a state-of-the-art bus terminal in a location where nobody wants to catch a bus. The concrete, steel, and the wages paid to workers; all of them have been procured at market value. But if you and I don't find it useful, all that spending doesn't create value. *(Connect the dots: Turn to pages 132–133.)*

Figure 3.1: A Diet Coke can

Why does a can of Diet Coke suddenly cost twice or three times as you are trying to get through the airport security? Nothing about that coke has changed. It's the same can, same fizz, the same Coca Cola brand, the same amount in the can even. No difference in quality either. Then, what has changed? Your options have changed. Outside the airport, you can walk to a kirana, pan shop, a supermarket or even order on Blinkit. Competition disciplines the price. But once you've crossed security, you are captive in that moment and can't step outside. If you want a cold drink before your flight, you're buying it here, at this counter, right now.

We think of prices as numbers on the back of a pack. But they are bits of information compressed as signals. The airport isn't expensive because diet coke is scarce. It's expensive because options are scarce. Prices don't reflect the cost of producing something as most people think they do. In fact, prices have nothing to do with the cost it took to produce that thing. With prices, the seller tries to get to the most you are willing to spend on it in that moment.

It appears most obvious but we forget it all the time. Think about it –

why is a glass of water practically free, while a diamond costs millions? Water keeps you alive; diamonds help you look good if you're wearing these. If value came from usefulness, shouldn't water cost more? But value comes from what people are willing to pay at that moment, not from how important a particular object is.

So, if value is just floating around in our heads, changing with our moods, circumstances and preferences, how does anything get bought or sold? How do millions of transactions happen every day?

The answer is simple – we don't need to agree on value. We just need to value things differently enough in order to engage in trade. The fact that we value things differently isn't a bug but a feature that makes trade possible. If we all valued everything identically, we would never ever exchange anything. Why would I give you my apple for your orange and vice versa if we both agreed they were worth exactly the same?

Thank You for Buying That Diet Coke Can at the Airport!

You must have been through the swanky new terminal 2 at the Bengaluru airport. Forest belt, open-air bridges, green walls, hanging gardens, and materials like ivory brown granite, umber red bricks, and traditionally woven rattan – it was pretty expensive to build!

Figure 3.2: Kempegowda International Airport, Bengaluru

These costs could, in theory,

be recovered by charging every passenger a higher ticket surcharge. But airlines resist that because it raises fares and pushes price-sensitive travellers to other modes of transport. So airport operators lease retail space at swanky airports at steep rents, and those rents are passed on to you in the form of an expensive Coke can, a ₹600 sandwich, and no deals on clothes. In other words, the passengers who buy things at the airport are quietly subsidizing the passengers who don't. This is also why popcorn at PVR costs more than the ticket itself!

What's a Fair Price?

Figure 3.3: A roadside dhaba

There's a *dhaba* near ITO where Akash sometimes gets lunch while in Delhi for work. Nothing very fancy – it has plastic chairs and tables with an overhead tin roof that drums loudly when it rains, smell of onions frying, clatter of steel plates and a very limited menu. The owner, Lal *ji*, serves exactly three things: *rajma-chawal*, *kadhi-chawal* and *chole-bhature*. Same price: ₹50 per plate, whatever you want.

Here's what happens every time Akash eats there. He hands over a ₹50 note. Lal *ji* gives him a steel plate with *rajma-chawal* (Baba Sehgal's song of the same name playing in his head). They both say thank you. They are both thanking each other for the same transaction!

In Akash's mind, that plate of food is worth much more than just ₹50. He's there, he's hungry, the nearest restaurant is a 15-minute walk away, and honestly, Lal *ji*'s *rajma* reminds him of his IIT hostel days. He'd probably pay ₹100 if he had to.

But here's the twist – Lal *ji* is equally genuine in his thanks. To him, that ₹50 note is worth more than the plate of *rajma-chawal* he just served. The ingredients cost him maybe ₹20, add *labour* and overhead, call it ₹30 all-in. He values that ₹50 more than keeping his *rajma*.

This isn't some economics textbook fiction but the reality of life. Akash is thinking, 'What a deal! Delicious home-style food for just ₹50!' Lal *ji* is thinking, 'Good, another ₹50, twenty more customers and I can pay today's rent.'

They 're both right. They both won. This is another one of your double thank-you moments, remember the last chapter?

> It is not from the benevolence of the butcher, the brewer, or the baker that we expect our dinner, but from their regard to their own self-interest. We address ourselves not to their humanity but to their self-love, and never talk to them of our own necessities but of their advantages.
>
> – **Adam Smith**, *The Wealth of Nations*[2]

The zero-sum mentality, which we call 'Kidonomics' is drilled into our heads from childhood – for someone to win, someone else must lose. We elaborate on this term in the later chapters. This thinking affects how we see business. 'Businessmen are exploiting customers.' 'Companies making profit implies consumers losing money.' 'If the shopkeeper is happy, I must have been cheated.' But voluntary trade isn't some monopoly board game from our childhood. That ₹50 transaction at Lal *ji*'s *dhaba*? It created value out of thin air. Akash valued the food at ₹100 but paid ₹50 – he gained ₹50 in personal satisfaction. Lal *ji* valued the food at ₹30 but received ₹50 – he gained ₹20. Together they created ₹70 of happiness that didn't exist before. Magic. *(Connect the dots: Turn to pages 117–119.)*

The principle holds even in transactions where you might have expressed more generosity than usual. When you tip the delivery boy extra during rain, think of it as buying the satisfaction of knowing he's compensated for the trouble. He's providing you the service of accepting your kindness. Both of you sleep better.

PRICE: THE SWEET SPOT WHERE MAGIC HAPPENS

So if Akash values Lal *ji*'s rajma at ₹100 and Lal *ji* values it at ₹30, why did they settle at ₹50? Why not ₹40 or ₹80?

Price is like the area where two circles overlap in a Venn diagram. One circle contains all the prices where Akash is willing to buy (anything below ₹100 for me). The other circle contains all the prices where Lal *ji* is willing to sell (anything above ₹30 for him). The overlap – between ₹30 and ₹100 – is where trade can happen.

But why specifically ₹50? This is where it gets interesting. If Lal *ji* charged ₹90, Akash would still pay. But countless of his customers wouldn't – the broke students from Lady Irwin College and School of Planning and Architecture or security guards who work at the University Grants Commission (UGC) office next door.

Similarly, if there were 50 *dhabas* on the same street and all were as good, competition might push Lal *ji*'s prices down to ₹35. The actual price depends on alternatives, information, bargaining power and a dozen other factors.

The beautiful thing is that anywhere in that ₹30–100 range, Akash and Lal *ji* both benefit. At ₹40, Akash gets a great deal and Lal *ji* still makes profit. At ₹80, Lal *ji* celebrates while Akash still gets food he values. The exact price determines how the benefits are split, but trade makes both better off regardless.

This is why haggling at Sarojini Nagar is so entertaining. When the shopkeeper quotes ₹500 for a *kurta* and you counter with ₹200, you're together trying to discover that sweet spot where you both win. He knows his cost, you know your budget, and through theatrical negotiation, you find a price where both of you walk away satisfied. But that haggling increases what economists call 'transaction costs'[3] – the time, effort and energy spent just to make a deal happen.

But not all exchanges are voluntary, and this distinction matters. When a thief takes your phone, that's not trade, but theft. The key ingredient for the magic of trade is choice. The ability to walk away. Before Akash eats at Lal *ji*'s *dhaba*, he has the choice to go to the restaurant down the street or pack lunch from home or skip lunch entirely. Lal *ji* could refuse to serve him and wait for other customers. This freedom to say no is what ensures both parties only say yes when they genuinely benefit.

So we have now established that trade happens because people value things differently, and prices emerge somewhere in the zone where both parties benefit. But this raises a puzzle. From Lal *ji*'s *dhaba*, now zoom out to the whole economy. Billions of people. 'Gazillion' items. Countless transactions every second. How are all these prices getting determined? How does your local vegetable seller know what to charge for tomatoes? How does Apple decide the price of its new phone? How does anyone know what anything should cost?

There's a hidden force determining where these prices end up landing. That something determines whether Lal *ji* charges ₹40, ₹50 or ₹60. Economists call it opportunity cost, but it is about murder! Flabbergasted? Let me explain.

EVERY CHOICE IS MURDER

It sounds dramatic, but think about it more carefully, and you'll see that it's true. Every time you choose something, don't you murder all the things you didn't choose? Economists have a boring name for this – 'opportunity cost'.[4] This concept is also behind *Murder at the Margin*, a mystery novel written by two US economists, William Breit and Kenneth Elzinga, under the pseudonym Marshall Jevons[5].

When Akash spent ₹400 buying magazines, his mother didn't just see the magazines. She also saw his brother's taekwondo classes vanishing. When his brother wanted that expensive cricket bat, she'd say, 'That is your brother's entire semester of books.' She was truly making the murdered alternatives visible. Every choice kills the other choices that could have been. This is the foundation of how prices work. Prices facilitate exchange between entire universes of possibilities. When you buy something, you are saying: 'Of all the infinite things this money could become, I choose this particular thing.'

Every price in the economy is actually many prices. The visible one on the label, and the invisible one – everything else that money could buy. When prices rise or fall, they are not only changing the cost of that particular item but also the entire constellation of choices available to people.

Now multiply these individual calculations by millions. Every person is weighing their options, every trader is calculating the alternatives they have and every business is choosing between possibilities they face. There are many opportunity costs fighting each other. How do all these separate decisions crystallize into actual market prices? To see this invisible process made visible, let us take you to where it actually happens in its most raw form.

Why Does Virat Kohli Earn More Than Rohit Sharma?

Figure 3.4: Virat Kohli (left) and Rohit Sharma (right)

In 2025, Virat Kohli reportedly earned over ₹200 crore from brand endorsements while Rohit's earnings from the same were estimated around ₹50 crore. That's a fourfold difference. So, does that mean Kohli is four times better at cricket? Their cricketing stats don't support this – both Kohli and Rohit have similar batting averages, both have won plenty of matches for India and both are undoubtedly legends of the game. If you were to compare pure cricketing 'value', they're quite comparable.

Then why is the earnings gap so massive? Because value is about what other people are willing to pay for it. Kohli's fitness videos, aggressive persona, marriage with Anushka Sharma, over 270 million Instagram followers – all of these come together with his cricketing skills and stats to create a unique value for brands. When Puma or MRF sign Kohli, they are buying his charisma. They think this cocktail has the potential to make millions of people want to buy their products.

The value you create (and hence what you earn) is not determined by your input. It is determined by what others get out of it. Rohit might practice just as hard, score just as much, but if fewer people are deciding to buy products because of him, his market value is not as much. Fair? Unfair? That's a different question. But that is how value works at the end.

HOW PRICES FORM

While researching for and thinking about this chapter, both of us (Akash and Kumar) went to Azadpur Mandi at 4.30 a.m. last month with our friend Raju, who runs a vegetable shop. The first thing that hit us as we reached wasn't the sight. Even before we got to the actual *mandi*, we could hear thousands of negotiations creating a roar that drowned the call to prayer – the *azaan* from the nearby mosque. As we got closer, we could smell the *mandi* – overripe bananas, all kinds of vegetables, diesel fumes and morning *chai*.

Figure 3.5: Azadpur Mandi

Raju got right down to business as soon as we got there. He approached a tomato wholesaler's truck. The truck was here from Nasik. The wholesaler who was still dusty from the overnight journey, started high: '₹25 per kg, *bilkul* fresh *maal hai.*'

Raju laughed. '₹25? Arre Bhaiya, last week, I had got even better tomatoes for ₹16.'

'That could have been last week. Diesel price has increased just this Monday, and then there was rain that damaged most of the crop in the region.'

'₹15. Final.'

'Are you joking? I won't even be able to cover my transport. ₹22 final.'

'Market *mein bahut maal hai*. ₹17, no more.'

They went back and forth haggling, the wholesaler occasionally turned to other buyers, Raju threatened to walk away twice. Finally: '₹19.50, done?'

'Done.'

Multiply this scene by thousands. Numerous trucks, all kinds of vegetables, infinite deals being made every minute. No central authority or computer algorithm setting prices. Just humans with incomplete information, time pressure and different needs and preferences negotiating. Somehow, by 7 a.m., a 'market price' for tomatoes emerged – around ₹19–20 per kg on that day.

How? The wholesaler started by checking what others were charging, adjusting his ask based on his desperation to sell before the market closes. Raju overheard conversation while walking past several trucks, mentally noting prices. A kind of collective intelligence then eventually emerged from individual haggles.

This is what economics calls price discovery. Nobody walked into Azadpur knowing tomatoes would settle around ₹19–20 at the end. That price emerged from thousands of individual negotiations, all building on information from each other. It is discovery in its finest sense – finding something that did not exist until the market created it.

The Textbook Version (Simplified but Useful)

If you're wondering how economists sleep at night looking at this chaos, here's our secret: elegant mental models that hold variables constant or omit complexities. Let me translate what the examples discuss in the language of economists, not because it's more accurate but because it's useful for thinking systematically about what moves prices.

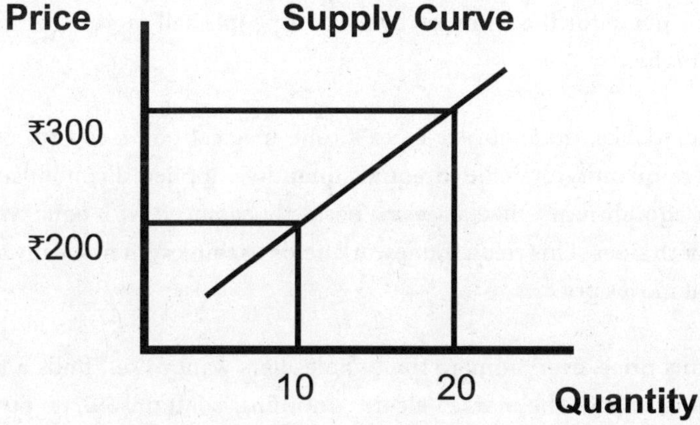

Picture all the vegetable sellers, hotel owners and household buyers who showed up that morning. Each has a maximum price they're willing to pay: Restaurant owners might pay up to ₹25 per kg (they'll pass costs to customers). Retail vendors like Raju can go up to ₹20 per kg (small margins). Household buyers directly won't pay over ₹23 per kg (they'll switch to other vegetables).

If you plotted this, you'd see demand falling as price rises. At ₹10 per kg, everyone wants to buy tonnes. At ₹30 per kg, only the desperate buy. This is the famous 'demand curve' – really just a fancy name for the common sense that people buy less when things cost more.

Now picture the wholesalers who drove through the night to reach Azadpur. Wholesalers with low working capital need to sell at any price above ₹15 per kg, maybe sometimes even at a loss while those with good quality storage facilities might even hold out for ₹20 per kg.

Plot this and supply rises with price. At ₹30 per kg, every wholesaler wants to sell everything. At ₹10 per kg, many would rather take their tomatoes back than sell at a loss. The 'supply curve' – again, just another fancy name for the common sense that people sell more when prices are higher.

In textbooks, these curves meet at one magical point, say ₹19 per kg where quantity demanded equals quantity supplied. Economists call this 'equilibrium'[6]– like a seesaw perfectly balanced with equal weight on both sides. This clean framework helps us think systematically about what moves prices.

At this price, every tomato that wholesalers want to sell finds a buyer willing to pay. The market 'clears' – nothing is left unsold, no buyer is left wanting. Except it is not really as clean in the real world. It works with the assumption that everyone knows the market price and all trades are taking place at that price. But truth be told, at 5 a.m., the Nasik wholesaler has zero idea what the Pune wholesalers are charging. Our friend Raju has no idea if tomatoes are better or worse three lanes away. There is a fair bit of guessing, bluffing and working with the small pieces of information that everybody has. Even after two hours, say at 7 a.m., when there is a rough market price that's starting to emerge, the trades are happening anywhere between ₹17 and ₹22. There are many factors behind this. Information travels slowly and gradually and the wholesaler at the far end of the *mandi* does not know if prices have dropped or risen at the entrance. In addition, the quality of produce varies and choices can be subjective – maybe plump tomatoes are going for ₹22, and slightly softer ones for ₹17. What Raju considers soft might be considered plump by another buyer. Add to that, negotiation skills and the buyer-seller relationships. Some buyers are simply better at negotiation than others. Regular buyers are likely to get better rates than strangers. It is also a function of urgency for buyers and sellers. Wholesalers who wish to complete trades sooner might accept less than those who can wait.

Next, we'll see how these prices coordinate the activities of complete strangers across the globe. But how does the tomato price in Azadpur Mandi connect to some farmer's planting decision in Nasik, a trucking company's route planning in Mumbai and your dinner plans in Bengaluru? It is because prices are not just random numbers – they are, as Hayek would call them, the nervous system of the economy.[7]

Prices Forming around You

So, as you see, the equilibrium that is studied by the economists is an abstraction but markets in the real world behave differently – always seeking balance, never finding it, and yet somehow working at the end. Whether it is Azadpur Mandi at dawn or Dalal Street in the afternoon, prices emerge from actions of innumerable individuals. Order from chaos, remember the first chapter? *(Connect the dots: Turn to pages 8-10.)*

1. **Your local *kirana***: Kushwaha*ji* is not consciously thinking about the 'demand and supply' concept. But when *dal* doesn't sell as much, he lowers prices. When Maggi is flying off all the shelves in his *kirana* and around, he adds ₹2 (Well, somewhat constrained by the MRP there, isn't he? Is that a good thing?). It is through trial and error that he finds prices that move inventory without leaving money on the table.

2. **Online markets:** Zepto and Blinkit change prices literally every few minutes, running experiments and conducting their A/B testing. Digital markets enable them to discover prices faster, but the fundamentals are the same – testing what people will pay, adjusting accordingly, and testing again.

3. **Stock markets:** Think Azadpur Mandi, but at warp speed. Instead of wholesalers and vendors, it's investors with different information, needs, and time horizons negotiating furiously without needing to speak a word to each other.

HOW PRICES COORDINATE STRANGERS

So far we have seen how prices emerge from chaos in individual markets. But that's not it. The individual markets are all connected with each other. So these locally discovered prices end up being part of the price discovery puzzle that coordinates activities across the entire planet. How does a price negotiated at dawn in Azadpur Mandi affect decisions in farms, trucking companies and restaurants far away across India?

When a drought hits Maharashtra, onion prices spike. Let us say they spike from ₹30 to ₹100 per kg – we only see the pain of the middle-class consumer on TV. But that spike is a signal for the whole market. That ₹70 spike is also interpreted, by some farmers in Nashik as a signal to plant more onions next season and by some cold storage owners to invest in bigger, better facilities. Some truck drivers construe it as onion routes being suddenly profitable and consumers substitute some of their onions with tomatoes. Think of every price movement as reshuffling the deck of human choices and doing so for innumerable individuals.

Rava Idli and the Magic of the Price System

The year was 1942. World War II was at its peak. Japan had just invaded Burma (Myanmar today). It had been almost two decades since the Maiya family had kicked off the operations at the Mavalli Tiffin Room, or MTR in Bangalore. MTR was built around crisp *dosas* and fluffy *idlis*, all made of rice batter. Most of the rice at the time came from Burma and thanks to the invasion, rice prices shot through the roof. Yagnappa Maiya, MTR's founder, was a smart man. He started experimenting with multiple ingredients. And it worked! He soaked semolina (*sooji* or *rava*) in curd, tempering it with mustard seeds and cashews in *ghee* and then steamed it just like he did his regular *idlis*. The result was the lighter and fluffier *rava idli*. Something that became so iconic with time that it only rose in popularity even after the war was over and rice was aplenty. Price signals redirect human ingenuity towards where it's needed the most. It made Mr Maiya reimagine the humble *idli*, and decades later, we are still marvelling at it.[8]

WHEN PRICE SIGNALS GET JAMMED

The miracle of the price signals seems almost too good to be true, so much so that we take it for granted and don't think about it too much. But what happens when these signals get jammed? *(Connect the dots: Turn to page 72.)*

The temptation that someone smart should oversee these signals and correct the inherent mistakes has seduced every government in history. The rationale? After all, how can you let these signals run amok – someone must ensure that the prices are fair and equitable.

Take the prices of onions that we were discussing in the last section. There are few prices as politically explosive as that of onions. When they spiked in 1998, it arguably cost the BJP the state elections in Delhi and Rajasthan. So, what do the governments do about it? The reflex is almost always the same – ban exports, release the buffer stocks and crack down on traders. That eases prices temporarily and the middle class feels some relief. The heat is taken off that election cycle. But don't forget what the higher prices were doing in the first place. They were a signal to the farmers to grow more onions, to the traders to improve cold storage and to the transporters to move supply where it was most needed. But that signal has been jammed so middle-class consumers can rest easy for now. What's the long-term result? Farmers play it safe, unsure if they'll get a better price next season or whether exports would be banned. Traders don't build new storage infrastructure. The next shortage always hits harder than the last.

Even today, with artificial intelligence (AI) and everything at its disposal, no computer can calculate the ever-shifting desires and preferences of billions of people for millions of products. But prices do it every second of every day. This was the subject of the socialist calculation debate in the 1920s.[9] The Soviet planners wondered why prices were even needed in the first place. The smart commissars could just calculate how much of everything people needed and produce that much. However, that would be a recipe for disaster. Every price is a message and millions of these messages coordinate human activity better than any planner ever could.

Is Hoarding Evil?

Pawan *ji* runs a cold storage facility in Bihar. In October, he noticed unusual rain patterns and asked around his farmer network. He figured there was some crop damage that was happening and predicted a requirement for onion shortage in the next two months. So he bought 50 tons of onions at ₹20 per kg and stored them.

Figure 3.6: Cold storage machinery

'This Pawan is a greedy hoarder!' said one of his neighbours when December came and onion prices hit ₹80 per kg. In fact, it was Pawan *ji*'s 'hoarding' that saved the neighbour from the onion shortage come December. By stocking it up; he was lending those onions to the future. Yes, he made money in the process and that is what motivated him to take that risk and smooth out shortages. Remove the profits and losses, and no one would do the hard work of predicting and preparing for future scarcity. The real villains are not the speculators but the government policies that prevent price signals from working. Under the Essential Commodities Act, 1955, onions are notified as an essential commodity.[10] The moment prices rise, government officials can raid Pawan *ji*'s warehouse, force him to sell at prices capped by the government, impose stockholding limits, and even jail him for 'hoarding'!

Now, think what that means. Pawan *ji* invested over ₹40 lakhs building that cold storage infrastructure, that too on credit that came at 12 per cent interest. Then he bought onions worth ₹5 lakhs and stored them. Had there been no shortages and prices went down, he could have lost money – both in terms of price and the opportunity cost of what else he could have stored in his cold storage. But his reward when he predicted the shortage correctly? Criminal prosecution!

Government reports lament at the lack of private cold storage infrastructure in the country while tying the albatross of criminal prosecution around those who build them. This is why India, a country that produces over 300 million tons of fruits and vegetables, has cold storage capacity for only 40 million tons. By some estimates, we even let ~30 per cent of our produce rot rather than store it, because the Essential Commodities Act makes storage a crime rather than a service that it should be seen as. As if this was not enough, when domestic prices rise, the government even bans onion exports to keep the prices low.

Had there been more cold storage facilities, enterprising farmers could have even rented some. But without adequate cold storage, they must sell immediately after harvest when prices are the lowest. During gluts, they watch helplessly as produce rots and during shortages, they're told they can't benefit from high prices. Remember how fast the government bans onion exports when prices rise? We have criminalized the very market mechanism that could solve price volatility.

The real tragedy in all of this is not that speculators profit, but that there aren't enough of them, thanks to the draconian Essential Commodities Act. Every missing cold storage facility represents millions of tons of wasted food and volatile prices that hurt both farmers and consumers. We've literally outlawed the solution to the problem we're trying to solve. It is like making the cure illegal and wondering why the disease persists. The 2020 farm laws were, among other things, an attempt to temper the Essential Commodities Act, if not repeal it completely.[11] But the government took it back under pressure.

The Price Cap Trap

Akash's house help, who is a diabetic, takes a medicine called Metformin. For years, she bought a particular brand for ₹3.50 per tablet. Then the government decided to help diabetics by starting to cap prices of essential medicines. Metformin 500 mg was legally required to cost less than ₹1.92 a tablet in 2021.[12]

'Great news!' She told Akash. 'My son told me my medicine just got cheaper!'

Six months later, her son was frantically searching every pharmacy in Bengaluru. That ₹3.50 brand had vanished. Completely. Like it never existed. Every pharmacist had the same sheepish explanation: 'Company stopped making it. Try this new one – same salt, better quality.'

Metformin 500mg forte with Vitamin B12 – ₹20 a tablet, the sustained release one for ₹12 a tablet, some fancy coating for a measly sum of ₹10 a tablet. While the original Metformin 500 mg by unknown new brands – that's for ₹1.92 a tablet, but good luck finding them. Welcome to the unintended magic of price controls. Latest we heard, government was planning to cap some combinations as well.[13]

But here's where it gets scarier. In 2017, the government capped stent prices at ₹30,000 (from ₹1.5 lakhs).[14] Another victory for patients, right?

Harshit's dad needed an angioplasty that year. The cardiologist pulled him aside: 'Look, I have to tell you something. The good stents – Abbott, Medtronic, Boston Scientific – they've either left India or stopped bringing their latest models here. At ₹30,000, they can't even recover costs. What we have now is either their 10-year-old models or local manufacturers whose quality... well, I can't vouch for it.'

'So what do you recommend?' he asked. The doctor looked uncomfortable. 'If you can afford it, medical tourism. Get it done in Thailand or Singapore where you'll get the latest-generation stents. Or take your chances with what we have.'

A policy meant to make heart treatment affordable instead created a two-tier system: rich Indians flying abroad for quality stents, poor Indians gambling with their lives on substandard ones.

Paying People to Dig Holes (and Fill Them Again!)

The government launched MGNREGA in 2005 to create rural employment. In a disputatious twist, it may have permanently eliminated more jobs than it created, building a system of dependence that grows stronger each year.

Figure 3.7 : MGNREGA Work

Last October, both of us were in a Bihar village during the paddy-harvesting season. Ramkishan, who farms five acres, was desperate. 'Nobody wants to work!' he told us. 'I'm offering ₹400 per day, still can't find anybody.'

Under MGNREGA, the government guarantees 100 days of work at minimum wage – about ₹250 daily. The 'work' often involves digging ditches that serve no purpose, building roads that already exist on paper or moving dirt from point A to point B, then back again.

We met Ramesh, a daily-wage labourer, at the village tea shop. 'Why not work for Ramkishan?' we asked. 'He's paying much more.'

Ramesh laughed. '*Bhaisahab*, in MGNREGA, I show up at 9 a.m., mark attendance and sit under a tree till 2 p.m. I still get paid. Earlier the clerk used to take the bribe. Now thanks to the direct benefit transfers, that has also reduced. But Ramkishan's field – that is some back-breaking work from dawn to dusk. Why kill myself for that extra ₹150 a day?"'

This conversation reminded us of economist Milton Friedman's visit to a government works project in Asia.[15] Seeing workers using shovels instead of machinery, he asked why that was the case. When officials explained it was to create more jobs, Friedman quipped, 'Then why not give them spoons instead of shovels?'

Digging ditches with no purpose except to justify payment is the same kind of bad policy that Friedman warned us against. Before MGNREGA, market wages for farm labour naturally fluctuated with seasons. During harvest, wages rose to attract workers. During lean periods, they fell but workers would find other tasks in construction, crafts or small trade.

Now? The ₹250 floor has destroyed these signals. Many farmers can't compete with MGNREGA. In the peak seasons, labour costs can spike to ₹700 per day and that is if they can find workers at all. Small farmers watch crops rot. Large farmers tend to mechanize faster, permanently eliminating jobs that once sustained villages.

But the deeper malaise is what economists call 'skill atrophy'. Why learn masonry? MGNREGA pays for digging holes is almost the same as what an apprentice mason would make for a much harder job. Why master carpentry or any specialized farm work? This is how a generation grows up seeing work not as value creation but as attendance marking. Economists like Jagdish Bhagwati and Arvind Panagariya have argued that if the government genuinely wanted to help rural workers, it could simply transfer ₹250 daily to their bank accounts and just waive the fake work required.[16] People could use that safety net while still taking real jobs, learning skills and creating value. The rural economy would have retained its natural price signals and seasonal rhythms.

Instead, we created the worst of all worlds. MGNREGA systematically dismantled the rural economy. In its place stands an artificial system where the government became the employer as the last resort, paying people to do unproductive work. If MGNREGA had to end tomorrow, there might not be a functioning rural economy to return to. The price signals have been jammed for so long that the market's natural coordinating mechanism has atrophied.

More Competition Means Fairer Salaries

Before we conclude that price signals are some kind of moral force, let us be clear – markets are amoral. They are tools. But interestingly, even this amoral tool can produce unexpectedly progressive outcomes. In the 1950s, economist Gary Becker came up with a model he called 'taste for discrimination'. His idea was that competitive markets would naturally eliminate discrimination. Not because businessmen would become enlightened, but because their taste for discrimination would become more expensive with competition.[17]

Imagine two equally skilled engineers – Rahul and Priya. A sexist employer refuses to hire Priya or offers her ₹50,000 while paying Rahul ₹80,000 for the same work. Subconsciously, what the employer is saying is, 'I'm willing to pay ₹30,000 extra to indulge my bias.'

Now enter a competitor (maybe an MNC) who doesn't care about gender. They hire Priya at ₹60,000 – she's thrilled (₹10,000 raise!), and they save ₹20,000 versus hiring Rahul. With lower costs, they can undercut the sexist employer. Over time, discriminating firms either abandon their bias or go bankrupt. We saw this play out in Indian IT. During 1990–2000s, when global tech companies desperately needed talent, Indian IT companies couldn't afford discrimination. Infosys, TCS, Wipro hired anyone who could code. Although that was a select group of people who could code at the time, we see that the representation of women, lower castes and small-town graduates rose steadily.

The caveat to add here is that price competition does not eliminate all discrimination – social biases run really deep. But it makes that discrimination costly. Every time you refuse to hire the best person due to irrelevant factors, your competitors who aren't doing so gain an advantage. This is why monopolies and industries protected from foreign competition often discriminate more – because they can afford to.

PRICE SIGNALS MIGHT NOT BE 'FAIR', BUT THEY ARE THE BEST WE'VE GOT

This isn't just theory. When labour markets get distorted, your food costs more. When medicine prices are capped, your parents can't find their diabetes drugs. When surge pricing is banned, you're stuck in the rain aggressively tapping on the Uber app. As an aside, the tipping before you even ride is a great innovation attempting to mimic the surge price but it adds transaction costs and keeps users guessing about the price point at which a driver would accept the ride.

Price controls hurt all of us. The next time you hesitate at a price tag, remember how many signals are encoded in that number. The dreams of Chilean miners, the calculations of Taiwanese engineers, the risks of cold storage owners – all crystallized in plain, simple digits. That's coordination on a scale that would make gods jealous. And it happens every second, in every market, without anyone in charge.

The question isn't whether prices are perfect. They are not. Perfect prices and perfect markets exist only in textbooks. Real markets are messy, human, and fallible. They overshoot and undershoot. They can be cruel and wasteful. The question is whether the alternatives are better. Those who want to play conductor in the symphony of the price system and assign us cues have failed every single time in history. The eternal, sanatan raga of the price system goes on.

KEY TAKEAWAYS

- Value is subjective. It comes from what others get out of it, not what you put into it.
- We trade because we value things differently. That difference is what makes trades possible.
- Every choice kills the alternatives. Opportunity cost is the true cost of everything.
- Prices emerge from messy negotiations, not a clean equilibrium.
- Price signals coordinate millions of strangers with nobody in charge.
- High prices scream 'make more', low prices whisper 'stop wasting resources'.
- Speculators and hoarders move goods across time. Criminalizing them worsens the very shortages we want to solve.
- Price controls don't eradicate the underlying problems. They silence the signals that would have solved them.
- The freer the price signals, the better the markets can coordinate human activity.
- Competition reduces discrimination.

4

WHY DO THINGS KEEP GETTING MORE EXPENSIVE?

Money and Inflation

♪ *Mehngai dayan khaye jaat hai* ♪

Last week, I overheard two aunties at the local *kirana* marvelling at the new ₹20 coin. 'So convenient!' one said, dropping it into her purse. 'No more fumbling with two tenners.'

Figure 4.1: ₹20 coin

But it's not just about convenience. If you think hard, it's a confession. The Reserve Bank of India just admitted that ₹20 has become so worthless, it now belongs in your pocket as *chhutta*, not in your wallet as real money.

When your parents got married, ₹20 could buy them dinner for two at a fancy restaurant. When you were in school, it was your whole week's *samosa*-and-*chai* budget likely. Today? It hardly gets you a cup of cutting *chai*. This chapter solves that mystery.

We spend our lives chasing money, saving money, spending money. But we rarely stop to ask what money actually is.

WHAT IS MONEY REALLY?

When Kumar was very young, there was a travelling ice-cream vendor who did business without a single rupee changing hands. His cycle rickshaw played that unmistakable jingle, but his real music was the rattle of grain. Kumar would run to his grandma for a steel container full of rice or wheat, which the ice-cream vendor carefully measured before handing over an orange bar.

Figure 4.2: An ice-cream vendor selling on the street at night

The ice-cream fellow preferred grain. He knew exactly what he could trade it for in the next village. Money is simply the thing we all agree to trade for other things. The grain worked perfectly because everyone in his circuit accepted it.

Who decides what becomes the medium of exchange? Just like no single person invented the language we speak, no single person invented the money we use. The emergence of money was not decreed by a king – it emerged because humans got tired of lugging goats to the market whenever they needed new pots or food. Throughout history, we see different societies coming up with different solutions: cowrie shells in coastal India, grain in agricultural villages, even cigarettes in prisons (more on that later).

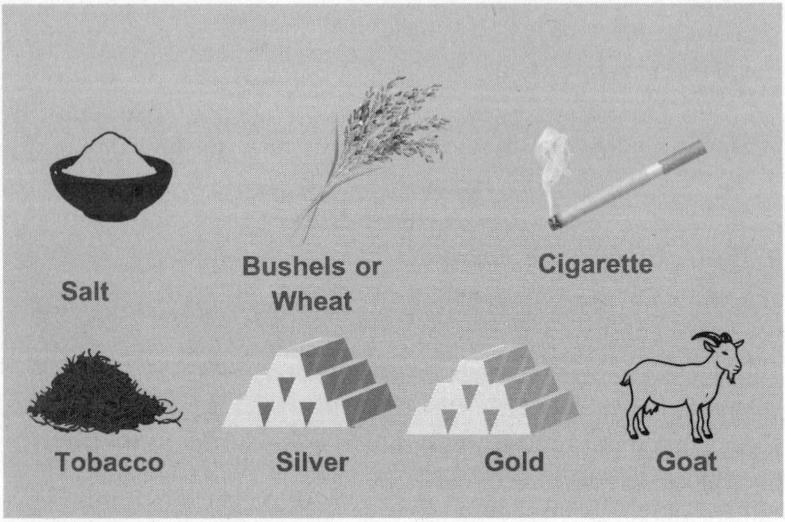

Figure 4.3: Goods used as money

Now take our ice-cream vendor in the story and transplant him to Mumbai. Picture him trying to pay his rent in rice or buying his lunch in exchange for orange bars. He would need to find a landlord who wanted rice at exactly the moment he needed shelter in exactly the right quantity. This is what economists call 'double coincidence of wants'.

Coins, rupee notes and now UPI – all solve this problem by making indirect exchange possible. Money becomes the universal translator of value that can convert your morning work into your evening dinner and even your month's labour into your car's equated monthly instalment (EMI).

Nobody planned this.[1] Money bubbled up from below, not top down. It's still evolving, going from coins and notes to cards, UPI and even cryptocurrency on your phone.

Cigarette Currency

During World War II, something remarkable happened in prisoner-of-war camps around the world. In absence of regular money, prisoners came up with their own economy with a fascinating new currency – cigarettes.[2] Even non-smokers accepted cigarettes because they knew others would accept them. Prices emerged naturally, a haircut cost two cigarettes, laundry service cost three.

Red Cross packages that would come to these camps would contain cigarette boxes, and whenever they arrived, prices would go up. When cigarette supplies ran low, prices came down. Nobody decreed it. No committee decided on these prices. Neither did the prisoners cast votes among themselves on these prices. It just happened on its own. That's the magic of money. It is not by government's decree that money becomes money, it is by its acceptance among people that it does.

THE FIVE TESTS OF PERFECT MONEY

Remember those double thank-you moments? *(Connect the dots: Turn to pages 16-17.)* They generally involve exchange of any good or service for a previously agreed sum of money. Thus, one half of almost all exchanges involve currency. Every time money changes hands, both parties should walk away satisfied. But for that to happen smoothly, millions of times a day, money needs to pass certain tests.

Good money is characterized by five qualities.

1. **Portability:** Gujarati diamond merchants carry crores worth of diamonds in shirt pockets – tiny stones worth more than most people's homes. Try that with cash. Even in ₹2000 notes, you'd need truckloads for a hundred crore. But cards and cheques solve that for larger volumes so you don't really need diamonds for large transactions.

2. **Divisibility:** You can't buy a ₹5 samosa with a ₹2000 note without change. Now imagine if your money was a piece of land. '*Bhaiya*, give me 2.5 square feet back as change!'

3. **Durability:** Salt was valuable in ancient times[3], but it catches moisture faster than Mumbai in monsoon. One humid day and your wealth dissolves. Your great-grandmother's gold bangles? Still shining after decades.

4. **Uniformity:** Every ₹100 note is identical. Every mango isn't. Imagine the chaos at Big Bazaar if the cashier had to evaluate the quality of each mango-currency. 'Sir, this one's too raw. Do you have a riper one?'

5. **Stability:** When onion prices swing from ₹20 to ₹200 in three months, nobody wants to be paid in onions. Your salary can't randomly become worth ten times less between morning and evening. But is the paper money in your pocket stable? Thankfully, much more than Zimbabwe in 2008. In months, a loaf of bread there went from costing under 1,000 Zimbabwean dollars to 1.6 trillion Zimbabwean dollars. Prices more than doubled every 24 hours. You'd negotiate your salary at breakfast and find it worthless by dinner.[4]

'Stablecoins' have tried to fix volatility by pegging to dollars. But what are they backed by? The crypto experiment is barely 15 years old. Too early to declare victory or funeral.

The Digital Money Experiment

In 2009, while governments printed money to fight the financial crisis, a mysterious programmemer called Satoshi Nakamoto created Bitcoin, money without a government. No central bank. No printing press. Just code.

Figure 4.4: Bitcoin symbol

How does Bitcoin score on our five tests?

- **Portability:** Perfect. Send ₹50 crores to Singapore in minutes for a few rupees.
- **Divisibility:** Excellent. Split it into 100 million parts. Buy ₹5 worth or ₹5 crore worth.
- **Durability:** Can't rot or rust. But lose your password? Gone forever.
- **Uniformity:** Every Bitcoin identical. No quality differences.
- **Stability:** Your cousin bought at ₹40 lakhs, watched it crash to ₹15 lakhs, then moon to ₹60 lakhs. It swings 20 per cent in a day. (But what if the people of Zimbabwe had access to Bitcoin a year before it was founded? Bitcoin's wild swings would've looked stable by comparison to their Zimbabwean dollars.)

Your Bank Account Is a Digital Hundi

Figure 4.5: Bombay Province ₹2500 Hundi

Long before your HDFC Bank passbook came to be, Indian merchants had solved a problem that stumped Europe. While European traders lugged chests of gold across pirate-infested seas, a Gujarati merchant in Surat could write a hundi – a piece of paper, and his cousin in Cairo would honour it.[5] No gold travelled. Just trust.

The Multani Shroffs ran history's first international banking network without a single computer. A trader could deposit silver in Delhi and withdraw gold in Constantinople. The Mughals used it, so did the British and today's bank transfers are basically digital hundis.

HOW DID WE GET TO THE RUPEE NOTE WE USE TODAY?

Figure 4.6: Bank of Bengal, ₹10, 1857

Here's something that would shock you. Before 1861, if you didn't trust Presidency Bank's notes, you could use Bank of Hindostan's. Or Bank of Bengal's.[6] It was like Uber versus Ola, but for money itself. Bad service? Your money isn't passing the five tests we discussed? Just use someone else's rupees. Then came the Paper Currency Act, 1861. Overnight, money became a monopoly. Only the British government could print rupees.[7] *(Connect the dots: Turn to pages 70–71.)*

Governments took control of money printing across the world. But there was still a leash, every note was a promise to pay gold. The Bank of England learned this the hard way in 1931 when France wanted its gold back and the bank couldn't pay. Time was ticking for the gold standard. By 1971, the game was up. Nixon shut America's gold window and the world followed. Your rupee became what economists call 'fiat money' – valuable because the government says so, not because it represents anything real.

Each step made some logical sense at the time. Each step also made it easier for governments to print. And print they did.

Mehngai vs Mudrasfiti

Open any Hindi newspaper's business section and you'll find headlines screaming about mehngai – how onions cost more, petrol prices are up, school fees have doubled. But Hindi, in its wisdom, has two words for this phenomenon. The word gathering dust in economics textbooks is mudrasfiti – literally, the swelling of money.

This linguistic split reveals something profound. Mehngai describes what you experience – things becoming expensive. Mudrasfiti explains why it happens – money bloating, becoming less valuable. Like a diabetic focusing on symptoms instead of blood sugar, we've been looking at the wrong thing. Among other things, the mainstream usage of the word inflation *to explain the rise in Consumer Price Index or Wholesale Price Index without an appreciation of the increase in quantity of money in circulation has led to wrong policy prescriptions.*

WHAT CAUSES INFLATION?

Imagine an island economy with just 100 people. They grow rice, catch fish and weave clothes – just the basics. For money, they use exactly 10,000 cowrie shells. That's all the cowries the island has. Over the years, prices have settled into some form of natural equilibrium. A kilo of rice costs 10 shells. A fish costs 5 shells. A shirt costs 20 shells. One fine day, a ship gets wrecked near the island. The islanders discover there's a chest of 10,000 cowrie shells this ship was also carrying. They are thrilled that they have found free money. The islanders are honest people so they divide it equally among themselves. Time to celebrate? Everyone's wealth has doubled overnight – except it hasn't!

Figure 4.7: An island

Remember the island still grows the same amount of rice, still catches the same number of fish and still weaves the same number of shirts. This newfound wealth is not going to increase the quantity of any of these. So, what happens when 20,000 shells chase the same goods that 10,000 shells were chasing before? Within days, the prices across all commodities adjust. Rice now costs 20 shells, fish 10 and shirts 40. All the prices just double. The end result is that the islanders are no richer than they were before. They have twice as many shells buying things that cost twice as much. *More money chasing the same goods always means higher prices.*

'But wait,' you say. 'The real world isn't an island with shells. What about droughts and wars? Supply chain problems?'

Let us add some complexity. The island's rice crop fails this year so they are left with only half the usual harvest. With the same money chasing less rice, rice prices should rise. But as islanders spend more on rice, they have less for fish and clothes. Demand for fish falls. Fish prices drop. The average price level stays roughly the same – just the relative prices (rice:fish:shirt) shift.

Unless ... someone finds another chest of shells. And here's where our island story meets the real world. Every crisis becomes an excuse for governments to create more money: When the rice crop fails, wouldn't it be nice to give farmers extra shells to survive? When storms damage the fishing boats, shouldn't we help fishermen rebuild?

Compassionate? Where do these extra shells or rupees come from? In the real world, they come from the central bank's printing press. The equation is simple. If you double the money but keep goods constant, prices double. If you print 10 per cent more money this year, prices rise roughly 10 per cent. Economist Milton Friedman summed it up: 'Inflation is always and everywhere a monetary phenomenon.'[8]

WHO KILLED THE RUPEE?

The Reserve Bank of India prints currency notes – it's one of the functions of the central bank. When and why they print new currency is key to understanding inflation.

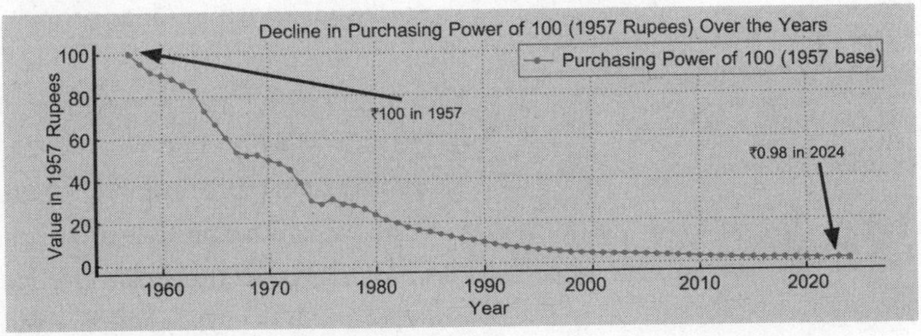

Figure 4.8: Falling purchasing power

The government has four ways to fund its spending:

1. **Tax** – Unpopular
2. **Borrow** – Limited by what markets will lend
3. **Sell** – Privatization of government assets might be prudential, but it is less popular
4. **Print** – Tempting and not really visible to the common man

When government spending exceeds its tax revenues and the capacity to borrow, printing becomes the easiest path in that moment. Here's the typical sequence:

A crisis looms – let's take the COVID-19 pandemic. Government announces relief measures. The bill comes to, say, ₹50,000 crores. Treasury doesn't have it. Raising taxes during a pandemic? Political suicide. Borrowing when markets are jittery? Very expensive. So the central bank creates new money. This new money enters the economy through government spending. More rupees now chase the same goods and services. Prices adjust upward in due time.

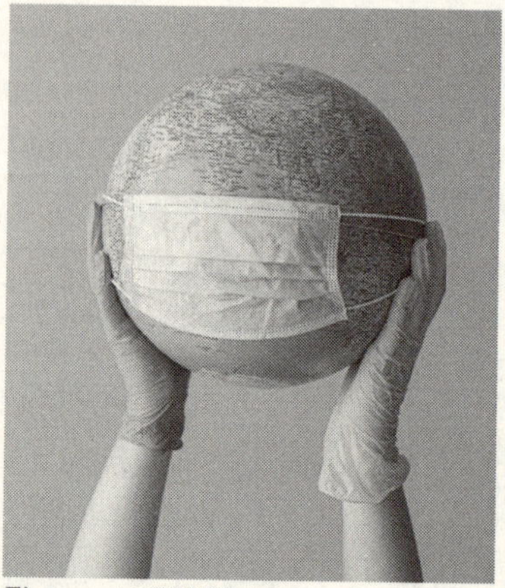

Figure 4.9: COVID-19

Since we took the example of COVID-19, it is worth noting that India's fiscal and monetary response to the pandemic was much more measured than say, the United States. From January 2020 to January 2022, the money supply increased in the United States by 40.1 per cent and in India by 22.6 per cent. The picture becomes much more dramatic when you take a look at the trend before the pandemic. So the 22.6 per cent growth in India's money supply over that two-year window was not negligible but was broadly in line with India's pre-pandemic trend, which was ~10–12 per cent annually. The United States on the other hand experienced a massive deviation – it basically added the money supply in just 2 years what it had in previous 14 years.[9]

Why did the United States print more? To give its citizens more money – the US fiscal stimulus was ~27 per cent of its gross domestic product (GDP), as opposed to India's ~10 per cent.[10] The United States could also afford to do so since the dollar commands a special place in the currency markets as the world's reserve currency.[11] The US borrowings are entirely in dollars. India's external borrowing is partly in dollars or other foreign currencies, so rupee depreciation makes that debt more expensive.

While the US Federal Reserve does have more headroom to print, the European Central Bank, the Bank of Japan and the Reserve Bank of India – all have printed trillions in recent decades. All their currencies have lost substantial value too. The technical term for this is 'monetary financing of fiscal deficits'.[12] The simple version: when governments spend more than they have, they print the difference.

So while Friedman said inflation is always and everywhere a monetary phenomenon, it can be argued that it is the fiscal needs that drive the printing. When governments need money they don't have, your savings pay the price through inflation. The question is, what can you do about it?

INFLATION AS THE INVISIBLE TAX

Every tax you know has paperwork. Income tax has returns. GST has bills and so on and so forth. There is that one tax which leaves no trace – inflation. The inflation tax works only because it is invisible. It takes 6–7 per cent of your money's value every year, and you never get a receipt for that. Think fixed deposits. That 7 per cent interest feels safe until you do the maths: deduct the 6 per cent inflation, subtract tax on interest, and you're left with ... almost nothing or even less than nothing at times. Your 'safe' investment is safely eroding. Or your salary. A 10 per cent raise sounds good until inflation takes its 6 per cent cut. Your real raise is just 4 per cent. But not everyone pays this tax equally. If you borrowed ₹50 lakhs for a home in 2014, you're repaying with 2026 rupees that are worth much less. Balle Balle if you are the borrower! But someone else's savings have funded that loan.

INFLATION AS A RUPTURE IN THE PRICE SIGNAL

Money does more than just store value. In the form of prices, it coordinates millions of strangers to work together as we learned in the last chapter. *(Connect the dots: Turn to pages 34–50.)*

Inflation ruptures this coordination. When the government prints money, it can send false signals. Say the RBI creates ₹50,000 crores to finance infrastructure spending and welfare payments. This money enters the system through government contractors or scheme beneficiaries. They rush to buy things at old prices. Prices rise in due time, but they don't rise uniformly.

Cement prices spike when the contractors buy cement first. Builders think it's real demand and they might take it as a signal to start more projects. Cement factories then expand production, hire workers and order machinery. But it's just new money working through the system. When the money flow stops, cement demand might crash. Factories will have to sit idle as a result, investments will turn worthless and workers will lose their jobs. It's like a game of passing the parcel, except the parcel is shrinking and the music here is inflation. When it stops, whoever holds the money loses the most.

The 2008 global crisis was partly this story. Cheap money from the Federal Reserve sent false signals about housing demand. Everyone built more houses. When reality hit, there was a bust.

Friedrich Hayek wrote about this extensively. Inflation scrambles the price system, which is the economy's nervous system.[13] Prices stop conveying facts on the ground and bad investments multiply as a result. The economy ends up producing things nobody really wanted. When money can't be trusted to hold value, prices can't be trusted to guide decisions.

The deepest damage caused by inflation arguably is not that it's a tax on savings, painful as that is, but the poisoning of the price signals that we learned about in the last chapter.

THE BOTTOM LINE

So, that ₹20 coin the aunty at the kirana found so convenient. Think of it as a quiet admission that the rupee has been slowly hollowed out over decades. Every new denomination is an epitaph for the purchasing power of the last one.

This didn't happen because rice became harder to grow or shirts became harder to stitch (actually, what happened was quite the contrary – thank technology). It happened because the money supply increased. Remember the price signals from the last chapter? The entire system that coordinates strangers across the planet, from Chilean lithium miners to your local kirana – that system runs on money holding its value. When the measuring stick itself keeps shrinking, every measurement it produces is a little bit off. Enough bad measurements, and the whole economy starts building things nobody needs with resources we can't afford to waste. So don't just ask 'Why is everything so expensive?' Ask: 'Did we print more money?"

Why Do Businesses Fail Together at Times?

In normal times, you see some restaurants closing down while new ones are opening up. Some shops are failing while others are thriving. That's healthy market competition. But sometimes thousands of businesses fail simultaneously. The 2008 crisis. The dot-com crash. Why does everyone make the same mistake at the same time?

The answer lies in false signals from manipulated interest rates. When the central bank artificially lowers rates at which money is lent to the market, it tells businesses that people want to save more for the future. Businesses invest based on this signal. But if people haven't actually changed their preferences then all those investments financed by the low interest rates might eventually fail together.[14] This boom-bust cycle is a sibling of inflation – born from the same monetary manipulation. But that's a story for another book altogether.

KEY TAKEAWAYS

- Money is not something that the government decreed into existence. It emerged spontaneously, just like language did.
- Good money has five qualities: portability, divisibility, durability, uniformity, and stability.

- Inflation is not prices going up. It is money losing its value. Mehengai, or price rise, is just the symptom. Mudrasfiti, or inflation, is the real disease.
- More money chasing the same goods always means higher prices. As Friedman remarked, inflation is always and everywhere a monetary phenomenon.
- Supply shocks change relative prices, not the overall price level. More money raises all prices.
- Governments fund spending through taxes, borrowing, selling assets, or printing. Printing is the most tempting because it is invisible to the common man.
- Think of inflation as the invisible tax. It takes from your savings but you never get a receipt.
- Inflation erodes savings. But more importantly, it poisons the very price signals that coordinate the economy, leading to bad investments and eventual busts.
- We cannot print our way to prosperity. Creating money without creating goods is creating inflation.

5

WHY DO SOME COUNTRIES GET RICH WHILE OTHERS STAY POOR?

GDP, Economic Growth and Institutions

♪ *Mere desh ki dharti sona ugle* ♪

You must have heard recently that India is on its way to become the third-richest country in the world. By now, dear reader, you know why we can't print our way to prosperity. It just can't be that the RBI will print us into being a $5 trillion economy! So, how do we tell whether a country is rich or poor? And what does it all mean for an average person?

How Do You Tell If a Country Is Rich or Poor?

The most well-known indicator used to compare two economies is the gross domestic product, or GDP.

WHAT IS GDP?

Much like your annual income, GDP is the *total value of all goods and services* produced in a country *in one year*.

Figure 5.1: What is GDP?

Imagine India as if it is like one big shop. Everything we produce in a year – rice, mobile phones, Bollywood films, IPL matches, Ola rides, hospital services, haircuts – it's all counted in the GDP.

WHY DO WE USE GDP AND NOT TOTAL WEALTH?

Wealth is a *stock variable* while income is a *flow variable*. Let me explain what we mean by both of these terms. A stock variable is calculated at a particular point in time. For example, how much money you have in your bank account today at this hour is a stock variable. A flow variable, on the other hand, is measured over a period of time. For example, how much did you spend from your bank account over the period of last month is a flow variable.

The total number of runs Virat Kohli has hit so far is a stock variable. The number of runs he hit during this IPL season is a flow variable. So this is also the difference between one's wealth and one's income. Your total wealth is accumulated money that you have but your total income is what you make in a given month or year. So, if you had to tell whether one person is richer than another, most people would compare the respective levels of wealth of the people in question and not their annual income. But that's not the case when we compare countries.

Why is that so?

The simple reason is that national wealth is much harder to measure and is often under-reported or informal in many cases. GDP, which is an indicator of national income, is standardized across countries and thus, makes it much easier to compare the different levels of national income. It also tells us how active or productive an economy is and how that is changing as it measures economic activity over time.

HOW IS GDP CALCULATED?

There are three ways GDP can be measured. They yield roughly the

What Is Not Counted in the GDP?

GDP only counts goods and services that involve a market *transaction* – that is, when money changes hands. But even all economic activity is not captured well in GDP. In developing countries, a large part of the economy operates informally. Street vendors, unregistered businesses, casual labour, or barter transactions often go unrecorded in national accounts. Although GDP calculations *attempt* to include such activities, the coverage is not complete or entirely accurate.

There's another service which isn't counted at all, since it's not a market transaction. If you cook a meal at home or care for your children, *no wage is paid*, and *no transaction is recorded*, even though valuable work is being done. Now, imagine you get tired of cleaning, cooking and caring for the pestering children. You start by ordering food for the family, hiring a maid to clean the house and send the kids to daycare. Suddenly, even though no new work is being done, the GDP increases. Why? Because money is exchanging hands and the same work is now paid for.

same result (allowing some wiggle room for measurement inaccuracies) because they're different ways of getting at the same thing. We can measure

1. everything we produce (all goods and services produced in India),
2. everything we earn (total income earned by everyone in the country),
3. everything we spend (total expenditure by everyone in the country).

Let's zoom into the third method. How do we measure all spends? These are the components that we add to get to the final number:

- Consumption (C) – People spending on things (clothes, food, petrol, haircuts)
- Investment (I) – Businesses investing in machines or buildings
- Net Exports (NX) – Foreigners buying Indian goods (exports – imports)
- Government spending (G) – Roads, defense and all the government schemes

So, GDP = C + I + NX + G

NOT ALL GDP GROWTH IS EQUAL

When you hear on the news that 'India's GDP grew by 7 per cent,' it sounds great – like the economy is booming. But here's the catch: *not all GDP growth is equal.*

When you look at C, I and NX, things counted in GDP are what people are actually paying for. But, when it comes to G, things are counted by how much it cost to make them, even if no one is buying them or they're given for free. Let me explain this with an example.

If the government spent ₹100 crores building a park no one goes to, it's counted in GDP.

But if a private company spends ₹100 crores making cars and only sells half, only the sales figures are counted. So government spending can artificially inflate GDP, even when real economic activity (jobs, incomes, business growth) is weak.

An increase in all four components – C, I, NX and G – show similar GDP growth, but they might not be equally healthy for the economy.

Next time you hear 'GDP grew by X per cent,' don't just stop there. Ask:

1. **Is private consumption growing?** Are people buying more stuff?
2. **Is investment rising?** Are companies building more factories or buying machines?
3. **Are exports increasing?** Are we selling more to the world?
4. **Or is most of the growth coming from government spending?** More subsidies, road projects or government salaries?

If the first three are strong, the economy is genuinely healthy. But if only government spending is going up, it's a warning sign, like applying make-up to a sick patient to make them look healthy.

CAR SALES ARE GOING DOWN!

Vehicle retail sales in India dropped by 7% in February 2025, reaching 18,99,196 units compared to 20,46,328 units in February 2024, according to the Federation of Automobile Dealers Associations (FADA) in a statement released on Thursday.[1]

Figure 5.2: Car sales are going down

We discussed that private consumption numbers matter for tracking meaningful economic growth. So, do decreasing car sales mean that the economy is in bad shape? Well, maybe. But not certainly. It is a *fallacy of composition* to assume that *what is true for one part is true for the whole.* So if car sales are falling, it might *look* like fewer people have money. But that might not be the whole story. Maybe people in metro cities are wondering, 'Why buy a car and pay for fuel, parking, EMI, insurance when one can just call an Uber or Ola in five minutes?'

So, if a particular industry is doing poorly – sales are low, people are losing their jobs, factories are closing down – it doesn't necessarily mean that the whole economy is doing poorly. That's why it's important to look at things holistically and not just go by media reports on any one industry. *(Connect the dots: Turn to page 7.)*

GDP IS GROWING BUT AREN'T THINGS GETTING MORE EXPENSIVE?

The simple answer is, *even if* things are getting more expensive, it is accounted for in the way we calculate GDP. Let's say you are an avid fan of *pani-puris* and you have one plate every week. Last year it was priced at ₹25 a plate, so you spent ₹100 a month. This year, in January, the seller hiked his prices to ₹30 a plate, so you're now spending ₹120 on the same four plates a month.

Figure 5.3: Panipoori stall

When Real GDP is calculated, the fact that you're paying more for the same thing is accounted for. Your *pani-puri* consumption contributed exactly the same amount to GDP both last year and this year. The way economists do this is by taking a particular year's prices as a benchmark and using this to take measurements for every year. That way you only see the change in actual output production, without fluctuating prices muddying the waters.

Nominal GDP, on the other hand, takes prices at face value. This means that in its calculations, last year's *pani-puri* consumption was ₹1,200 while this year's is ₹1,440.

The important thing to always remember is GDP comparison is *only ever made* between Real GDP figures. That means when you hear that we saw X per cent growth in GDP last year, we are talking about a real growth in output, unadulterated by any changes in price. Inflation (rising prices) might have many other problems, but accurately measuring GDP growth is not one of them.

BUT AREN'T THE SAME THINGS MORE EXPENSIVE IN SOME OTHER COUNTRIES?

₹100 in India might buy you a meal or a haircut but the same value might not even get you a pack of chewing gum in the United States. So, does GDP account for that? No, it doesn't. When we compare GDP between countries, we use the exchange rate as is. However, we do have another measure to capture this nuance: purchasing power parity (PPP).

PPP adjusts the GDP based on *what people can actually buy* in their own country. It compares how many goods or services people can buy, not just how much money those goods or services cost. In 2024, India's GDP was $3.9 trillion while the United States's was $29 trillion (World Bank data). But India's PPP-adjusted figure was around $14 trillion, which is just about half the American number.

DOES THAT MEAN THE US IS ONLY TWICE AS RICH AS INDIA?

While we are comparing countries, GDP and PPP can help us understand what a country produces and serve as a proxy for national power. Yet it tells us nothing about how the average person in the country is doing because it's not adjusted for population.

While American PPP might only be twice India's, the US population is ~340 million, i.e., less than a fourth of ours! When we divide by population, even taking PPP, the per capita income in India is still approximately eight times less than that in America. If we compare GDP, that figure looks more like a 26-times difference. The same phenomenon holds true when comparing the GDP of the United States and China. Although the numbers seem to be converging, it's important to remember China also has four times as many people as the United States.

Does it mean more population leads to more division of GDP and thus more poverty? Stick till the end of the chapter to find out.

While GDP per capita or PPP per capita are better indicators of what the average person's standard of living is, one might ask what they tell us about the income spread between the rich and the poor. The answer? Mostly nothing. *(Connect the dots: Turn to pages 120–122.)*

A Big, Juicy Lesson in Economics

Economics can get dry until you bite into a Big Mac. Imagine walking into a McDonald's in New York. A Big Mac demands $5.50, no ketchup packets included. In Delhi? That same burger royalty (Maharaja Mac) bows down for just ₹250.

Figure 5.4: Burgers

If life were fair, ₹250 would magically equal $5.50. Spoiler Alert: It doesn't. Welcome to the wild world of PPP! The Big Mac Index is quite a yummy way to understand global money power. Invented by the *Economist*, it asks: How much burger does your buck buy? This burger magic is a fast-food version of what we just learned with PPP. And when you apply PPP to a country's total income, you get *PPP per capita*: how rich the *average* citizen *feels*, not just how rich the country *looks*.

GDP is the big kitchen but PPP per capita is what's actually on your plate.

> In fact, the Big Mac Index underestimates the real differences in PPP. While a Big Mac in the United States is a mass-market product and represents an average meal, a Maharaja Mac in India is a semi-premium product that doesn't represent the meal of a median person.[2]

WHAT ABOUT EDUCATION AND HEALTH?

In 1990, another index debuted claiming to be a better indicator of how good life was in a particular economy. At the time Amartya Sen was writing about his idea of what true development meant,[3] he argued that it wasn't just about having money, but people's freedom and ability to live a good life: being healthy, being educated, and participating in society.

Mahbub ul Haq, inspired by this approach, devised the human development index (HDI) that was based on equally weighting three indicators: income (GDP per capita), health (measured by life expectancy) and education (measured by mean and expected years of schooling).

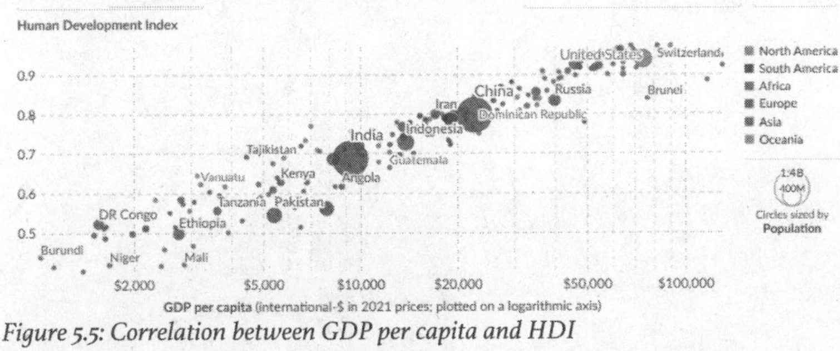

Figure 5.5: Correlation between GDP per capita and HDI

Richer countries almost always have better healthcare, higher levels of education, and longer lives. So *when GDP per capita rises, HDI usually rises too* even if not always at the same speed.

There are plenty of issues with HDI though. One-third weightage each to income, health and education indicators is arbitrary. More so, it uses a log scale while taking income into account. What does that mean you might ask? Without going into the mathematics of it, consider a simple example. Think of a staircase, you'd imagine its steps to be of the same size each. But think of the staircase if it were to follow the log scale as this – as you climb up the staircase, the steps get smaller the higher you go.

Imagine a country's income doubled next year and everybody just became twice as rich. In HDI, the 'income' score only increases a *little bit*, so even a huge surge in economic growth might just barely budge HDI. It is a 100 per cent growth rate year-on-year but not much HDI growth to show for!

Good Vibes, Bad Data

Measuring happiness with surveys is like measuring love with a thermometer.

Figure 5.6: Happiness in Bhutan

Bhutan showed up to the GDP debate and said, 'Forget money. Let's measure happiness!' Thus was born *Gross National Happiness (GNH)*.[4]

Bhutan decided their success

wasn't how much stuff they produced but how many smiles they could collect. They created a happiness formula with ingredients like

- how clean the air is,
- how many friends you have,
- how many hours you sleep,
- whether you feel *spiritually fulfilled* ... (we're not making this up).

The rest of the world followed it with countless *World Happiness Reports*. But you can't just toss people's feelings into a blender, add two parts income and sprinkle 'trust in government', to pour out a happiness smoothie.

Happiness is extremely personal. Different cultures understand and express happiness differently. So, when you ask people in Norway and in Russia, 'How happy are you?', people's interpretation of the same question varies wildly and thus, the answers are subjective and not easy to compare fairly.

Trying to squish something as complex, personal and emotional as happiness into a neat, global number just doesn't make much sense. Happiness isn't a number. It's a messy, beautiful human experience that no survey can really capture.

HOW MUCH DOES ECONOMIC GROWTH MATTER?

My life has been a product of compound interest. – **Warren Buffett**

Over the last few years, you've probably heard that India has been the fastest-growing major economy in the world. So, how much does that matter? It turns out, quite a lot. Without sustained growth, everything else – health, education, happiness – becomes a fight for scraps. With growth, you have a bigger cake to slice for everyone.

The reason growth matters so much is simple: *it compounds*. When an economy grows at 6 per cent a year, it *doubles* in size roughly every 12 years. At 8 per cent? *Every 9 years!*

Between 1980 and 2020, China's economy grew by about *10 per cent per year* on average. How much does it compound to? It means the Chinese economy was about *45 times larger* in 2020 than it was in 1980.

That's the magic of compounding: *small differences in growth rates today explode into giant differences in wealth tomorrow.*

The last century of economic data tells us that it's easier for a poor country to grow at a faster rate than a rich one, since there are many low-hanging fruits in terms of how the economy operates. It's called catch-up growth in economics, and it presumes rich and poor countries will converge over a period of time.

Yet once countries start getting richer, it becomes ever more difficult to keep the economic growth rate up. This phenomenon is called the 'middle income trap', a situation where a country's economy stagnates and is unable to move to a high-income level. Considering how hard-won economic growth is, especially for countries that have fewer of these low-hanging fruits, it is worth pondering over the credibility of an index like HDI which 'flattens' the effect of growth at higher levels.

> The elementary mathematics of compound interest is one of the most important models there is on earth. – **Charlie Munger**

WHAT CAUSES ECONOMIC GROWTH?

> *Is there some action the government of India could take that would lead the Indian economy to grow like Indonesia's... ? If so, what, exactly? If not, what is it about the 'nature of India' that makes it so? The consequences for human welfare involved in questions like these are simply staggering: Once one starts to think about them, it is hard to think about anything else.*[5]

So wrote Nobel Laureate economist Robert Lucas in 1988. Indonesia, under Suharto, had implemented pro-market reforms and was experiencing rapid GDP growth. (The fact that it went downhill from there some time later is a different matter altogether). India, on the other hand, was still a quasi-socialist economy, heavily regulated under the 'licence *raj*'.

What makes economies grow? Why do people in some countries earn much more than those in others? Can governments do anything to change this? These are questions that interest both economists and everyday people. Traditional economic models say growth comes from building up capital (things like machines, buildings), skilled people, and new technologies. But these are just surface-level answers. They don't explain why some countries have more of these things than others.

Is Overpopulation the Root of Poverty?

When we say overpopulation, we often imagine more people fighting to consume a finite pool of resources. But that's not a very sophisticated way to think about things.

Every person also has *two hands to work* and a *brain to think and innovate*. With the right opportunities, people contribute far more than they consume.

> *'The ultimate resource is people – skilled, spirited, and hopeful people who will exert their wills and imaginations for their own benefit, and so, inevitably, for the benefit of us all.[6]'*
>
> ***– Julian Simon***

Singapore is one of the most densely populated countries in the world, and also one of the richest. The Netherlands has a higher population density than India, but their people enjoy high incomes and good living standards. Meanwhile Bangladesh is also very dense, but not very rich. So some densely populated countries are rich, yet some are poor.

Figure 5.7: Chinatown in Singapore

Country	Population density (per sq. km)	GDP per capita (2025)
Singapore	8120	$93K
Bangladesh	1333	$2.7K
Netherlands	541	$70K
South Korea	530	$38K
India	488	$2.9K

Australia and Canada are some of the most sparsely populated countries in the world – yet they're fairly rich. The United States is also not very densely populated, but very rich. While some other sparsely populated countries like the Central African Republic and Chad are among the poorest in the world.

Figure 5.8: Bangui, Central African Republic

Country	Population density (per sq. km)	GDP per capita (2025)
Australia	3.5	$65K
Canada	4.5	$54K
Central African Republic	8.6	$0.5K
Chad	16	$1K
USA	38	$89K

One thing worth noting is that even the rich countries that seem sparsely populated hide density beneath the surface. Nearly 90 per cent of Australia's population lives in urban areas and within 50 kilometres of the coastline – that is, in 3 per cent of the total landmass of the country. Major cities in Canada – Toronto, Montreal and Vancouver – all have population densities over 4,000 people per square km. New York City's population is greater than that of the 10 least populated US states put together.

Meanwhile in the Central African Republic and Chad, most of the population lives in rural areas and is too dispersed across the country to build viable infrastructure. *To sum it up, it's not about how many people live in a country. It's about what opportunities they have to be productive.*[7] *(Connect the dots: Turn to page 98.)*

Do Natural Resources and Geography Make a Country Rich?

Australia and Canada have too few people, but a lot of land and an abundance of mineral resources. It might give an impression that if a country has abundant natural resources, it is destined to be rich.

Yet natural resources alone are often not the key to prosperity. Sometimes, having too much might even prove more a burden than a blessing. Nigeria and Venezuela sit atop enormous oil reserves. The Democratic Republic of Congo has immense wealth in minerals, including diamonds and cobalt. Yet these countries struggle with poverty, corruption and political instability. The presence of resources, instead of fostering prosperity, seems to create conflicts, poor governance, and economic instability.

Economists call this puzzling situation the *resource curse*. It describes how resource-rich countries without proper institutional frameworks often suffer slower economic growth, higher corruption, and worse outcomes for their citizens.

Singapore and South Korea, both rich countries that we discussed above, have very few natural resources. Singapore became incredibly wealthy due to trade, innovation and good governance while South Korea built its prosperity on high-end manufacturing and services.

In the distant past, geography, just like access to rivers or fertile land, helped some civilizations grow. But once those advantages disappeared, many of those societies declined. Today geography still matters, but it isn't enough to explain why some countries become rich and others stay poor. Both Haiti and California face earthquakes and natural disasters of similar magnitudes, but California recovers better because it has more money and stronger institutions.

Natural resources and geographical aspects are not the most decisive factors in wealth creation.

Wager of the Century

Figure 5.9: Simon-Ehrlich Wager

In 1980, economist Julian Simon and environmentalist Paul Ehrlich made a famous bet. Ehrlich argued that the earth's resources were being rapidly depleted, leading to scarcity, rising prices and disaster. Simon disagreed, believing human innovation would always find substitutes or new methods to produce resources, making them cheaper over time.

They chose five metals (copper, chromium, nickel, tin and tungsten) and bet on whether their prices would rise or fall over the next decade. Ehrlich predicted scarcity would drive prices up. Simon said they would fall, trusting human ingenuity to outpace scarcity.

Ten years later, in 1990, the results were in: *prices had fallen significantly*, and Simon won the wager. This story powerfully illustrates a fundamental truth: **human innovation and wise governance, not merely resources, create enduring wealth and prosperity.**[8]

Must It Be Colonialism?

Recall the hockey stick of human prosperity discussed in the first chapter. Most of the world was poor and had terrible living conditions till around 1800. Now juxtapose that with the things that you may have heard about India being the *sone ki chidiya* and having the lion's share of the world economy, around 20–25 per cent until somewhere around 1750.[9]

It's only when you look at both these graphs together, that the real picture becomes clear. It's not (just) that India was exploited by the British and became poor. Instead, the more pertinent factor in India's decline in the share of global GDP is that the Western world became incredibly rich in the aftermath of the industrial revolution. *(Connect the dots: Turn to page 114.)*

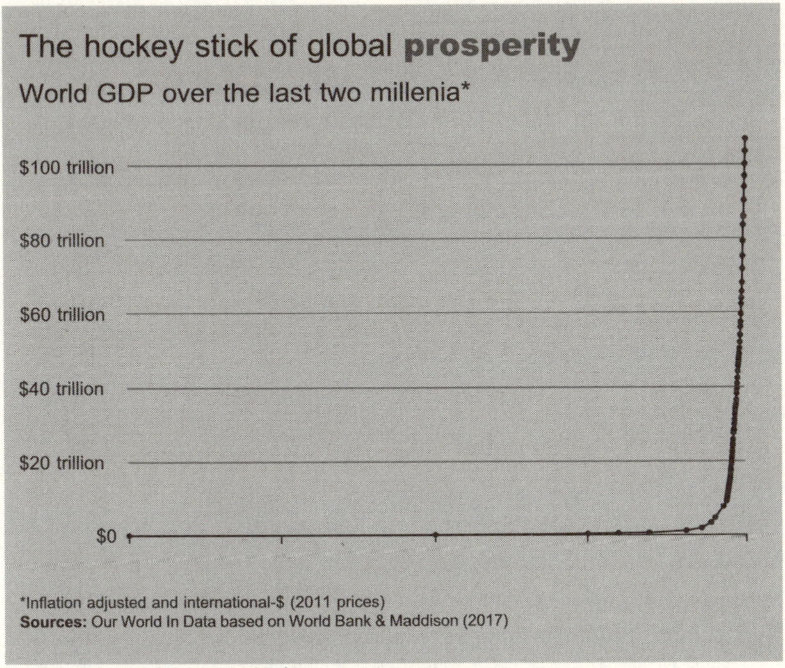

Figure 5.10: The hockey stick of human prosperity

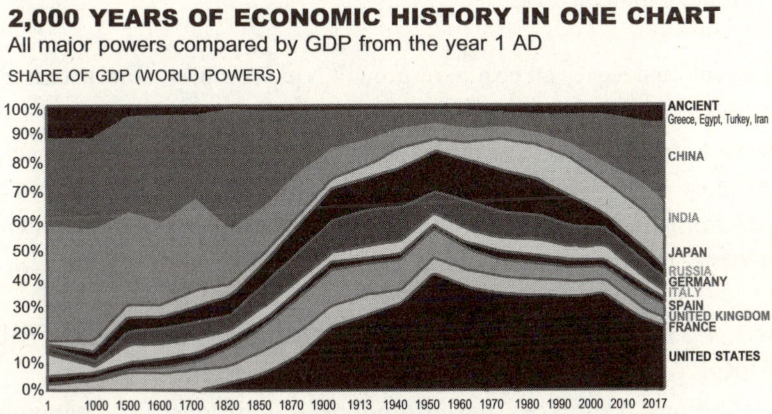

Figure 5.11: 2000 years of economic history

Country	Connection w/ colonialism	GDP per capita (2025)
Switzerland	Never held significant colonies	$106K
Singapore	Former British colony	$93K
USA	Never held significant colonies	$89K
Hong Kong	Former British colony	$56K
UK	Former major colonizer	$52K
South Korea	Former Japanese colony	$38K
Spain	Former major colonizer	$36K
Portugal	Former major colonizer	$30K

The table above tries to shed some light on how former colonizers, non-colonizers and colonies fare today in terms of per capita income. Some former colonies have done very well, but so have countries like Switzerland and the United States that held no significant colonies. Meanwhile, major colonizers like Spain and Portugal are closer to middle-income countries than to the United States today in terms of their per capita income.

The colonial legacy on economic growth is too complex to be discussed in this book, but to explore this further, you may read *The Economic History of Colonialism* by Leigh Gardner and Tirthankar Roy. This much is clear: After decades of independence, it's unreasonable for most governments of former colonies to solely blame colonialism for their persistent underdevelopment.

SO, WHAT MAKES A COUNTRY RICH AND ANOTHER POOR?

Institutions, institutions and institutions, as the Nobel Prize winning trio of Daron Acemoglu, James A. Robinson and Simon Johnson would put it. But what are these institutions?

Institutions are the rules of a game that everyone in a country plays. These rules decide who gets what, who makes decisions and how people can earn and grow. If the rules are meritocratic, predictable and allow everyone to play, the country does well. If only a few control the game, they might fare well, but the whole country loses out. That's the core premise of the widely celebrated bestseller *Why Nations Fail* by Acemoglu and Robinson.[10]

The primary reason countries become rich or poor is the way their governments and systems are set up; not their location, culture or how smart their leaders are. If a country has *fair rules where people can own private property, freely innovate and do business and count on the rule of law*, it usually grows richer. These are called *inclusive institutions*. But if a small group of people control all the power and wealth and are able to make rules to keep those power structures in place, the country stays poor. These are called *extractive institutions*.

But how do these inclusive institutions come up in the first place? Can you just copy them from one country and paste them into another? Raghuram Rajan notes that simply calling for good and inclusive institutions doesn't amount to constructive policy advice. Institutions aren't just written laws! They include habits, trust in society, power structures and what people actually *do* in real life. Just telling countries to 'build good institutions' is like telling someone to 'be healthy' without showing them how, especially when their environment doesn't support it.[11]

Joel Mokyr was awarded the 2025 Nobel Prize in economics for enriching our understanding of the cultural and civilizational aspects that lead to economic growth.[12] According to him, economic growth happens when people who *understand* how things work (scientists) connect with people who *make* things work (engineers, craftspeople). Innovation is a result of these two worlds coming together and talking to each other. This is the fundamental argument of his book *The Gifts of Athena* (2002).[13]

Figure 5.12: Joel Mokyr, 2025 Nobel Laureate in Economic Science

Now, at this point, we must pause and ask: how and why did this first happen in Europe? Mokyr answers this in *A Culture of Growth* (2016). He argues that Europe developed a competitive marketplace of ideas where thinkers across disciplines and countries challenged each other, shared findings, and built a culture that valued progress and practical knowledge.[14] A similar argument is made by Deirdre McCloskey in *Bourgeois Dignity: Why Economics Can't Explain the Modern World* (2010). She argues that what really drives economic growth is a change in *ideas,* and how people view business, success or innovation. Europe didn't grow rich just because its rules changed. It grew because its people's thinking changed. They started respecting entrepreneurs and wealth creators. It was the mindset shift and not just the new rules that drove the industrial revolution.[15] *(Connect the dots: Turn to page 113.)*

The question remains: what was so special about Europe that this happened there first? At the risk of digressing and going beyond the scope of this book, we'd briefly discuss one of the most fascinating explanations for this question. In *The WEIRDest People in the World* (2020), Joseph Henrich argues that it was a complete accident. The

Catholic Church, in its bid to consolidate power, ended up rewiring the European psychology. The medieval church banned cousin marriages, broke up clans and discouraged extended family networks – structures that were norm across the world at the time. It did so because it was important to weaken and dismantle those tight kinship structures to become the sole entity with a totalitarian presence in the individual's life. But doing so the medieval church forced Europeans to build trust with strangers and join voluntary associations. Over the next few centuries, it produced a peculiar psychological profile of people in Europe: individualistic, rule-following, guilt-driven and oriented towards impersonal institutions. These mental shifts laid the groundwork for Europe's economic take-off.[16]

So, when you hear policy ideas being debated, ask yourself this: Is this going to grow the country's economic pie so that everyone can have more? Or is it going to pit people against each other for the limited number of small crumbs that exist today?

KEY TAKEAWAYS

- GDP measures a country's income, not its total wealth. GDP is the value of all goods and services produced in a year.
- Not all GDP growth is equal. A rupee of growth from private consumption or investment is not the same as a rupee from government spending, even though the GDP number you see treats them similarly.
- Falling sales in one sector doesn't necessarily mean the entire economy is weak.

- Real GDP strips out inflation, giving a truer picture of actual economic growth than nominal GDP.
- GDP per capita, especially when adjusted for Purchasing Power Parity (PPP), is a better indicator of how the average person is doing than total GDP.
- GDP Per Capita is not a perfect measure of a country's well-being, but it's by far the best one we've got. Alternative indices like HDI and GNH try to go beyond GDP, but bring bigger problems: arbitrary weights, subjective surveys and flattened growth effects.
- Sustained economic growth compounds powerfully. Small differences in growth rates today explode into gigantic differences in wealth tomorrow.
- Poor countries can grow fast by picking low-hanging fruit, but sustaining that growth gets harder as they grow – something known as the middle income trap.
- More people don't mean more poverty. It is what people are enabled to do that determines prosperity.
- Natural resources do not guarantee wealth. Some of the richest countries have almost none; some of the poorest are sitting on enormous reserves.
- Even if colonial legacy had some influence, continued underdevelopment after decades of independence cannot be explained by colonialism alone.
- Rules matter more than resources. Inclusive institutions like property rights, rule of law, fair governance, lead to prosperity. Extractive ones keep countries poor.
- Good institutions can't just be copy-pasted. They grow from culture, trust, habits and how people actually think about enterprise and innovation.

- Ideas drive growth. The countries that got rich first did not simply change their rules. They changed how people thought about progress, business, and wealth creation.
- Once you start thinking about what causes economic growth, it is hard to think about anything else because the consequences for human welfare are staggering.

6 WHY DO SOME PEOPLE GET RICH WHILE OTHERS STAY POOR?

Innovation, Inequality and Entrepreneurship

♪ Jo Jeeta Wohi Sikandar? ♪

WHAT IS INNOVATION?

When you think of innovation, it's very likely that flying cars, robots or some breakthrough technology comes to your mind. But most real innovation is much simpler. *Innovation is about finding new ways to create more value from the same inputs.*

Figure 6.1: An Uber car

Take Uber's example. Did they invent cars? No. Did they invent mobile apps? No. Did they invent the Global Positioning System (GPS)? No. Taxis have existed for almost a century now. Smartphones were already in people's pockets for a while. GPS was already telling us where to go. What Uber did was connect these existing pieces in a novel way.

Before these apps, a taxi driver would roam around looking for passengers, burning fuel and wasting time. Passengers would stand on the road, hoping an empty taxi would pass by. The cars were already there, so were the drivers and the passengers. But a lot more time and fuel were wasted. Now? The app connects them instantly. The driver knows exactly where to go. The passenger knows exactly when the ride will arrive. *Same inputs, but much more value being created.* Innovation is not always about inventing something completely new. More often, it is about using existing resources more efficiently, combining old things in new ways, eliminating waste in the system or even solving problems people didn't realize they had.

Remember when you had to go to a restaurant to order food? Swiggy and Zomato just decided that you'd like it if they brought the restaurants to you directly. They didn't invent restaurants, delivery executives or motorcycles. They just connected them differently through an app. Suddenly the same kitchen could serve many more customers without adding a single table. In the cases of cloud kitchens, even without having a single table.

You don't always need to be a scientist in a lab coat to innovate. You just need to look at what exists in the world around you and ask, 'How can we get more value from this?' Sometimes the answer is a new technology. But often, it's just a better way of doing things we are already doing.

Why Don't Big Indian Companies Innovate More?

India's top private companies spend less than 1 per cent of their revenue on R&D, while global tech giants spend upwards of 10–15 per cent.[1] Are Indian businessmen less creative? Not really.

When you're protected by high import duties, complex regulations or licences that keep both new entrants and foreign competition out, why think of doing anything novel? If customers are stuck with just a few domestic alternatives, why improve? R&D is risky and expensive. It's much easier to keep selling the same product when customers have limited choices.

Look at what happened when markets opened up. Take Bajaj! '*Hamara* Bajaj' was so protected that getting one required either contacts or a decade-long wait. When competition arrived, did Bajaj die? No, they evolved. Today they are one of the largest two-wheeler companies in the world. Competition didn't kill them; it made them stronger. (Fun fact: Rahul Bajaj, along with other industrialists of 'Bombay Club' opposed the opening up of the markets.[2])

When private airlines were finally allowed, Air India had to start caring about its on-time performance. Its newly minted competitor, IndiGo, briefly emerged as not just India's but one of the world's most valuable airline companies by market cap within two decades of inception.[3] Protected markets breed complacency. *Competition and market discipline force innovation.* This is why the most innovative sectors are also the most competitive.

WHAT IS ENTREPRENEURSHIP?

Entrepreneurs start businesses, but what do they actually *do*? They imagine things that do not exist yet and figure out ways to create them.

Imagine you notice people in your neighbourhood struggling to get fresh vegetables. The nearest market is 5 km away. You think, 'What if I start delivering fresh veggies to their doorstep?' This service does not exist yet and you are imagining something new. Will people pay for it? How much? You have to figure all of this out. This is what entrepreneurs do. They spot gaps between what exists and what could exist. Maybe it is a new product ('What if we made instant *dosa* batter that actually tastes like homemade *dosas*?'). Maybe it is a new process ('What if we could recycle temple flowers into incense sticks?'). But it is about creating something that does not exist today.

To start your vegetable delivery service, you need a second-hand van (₹5 lakhs), a driver (salary ~₹15,000 per month), cold storage (~₹2 lakhs) and some supply of vegetables. Others want these same resources. Maybe someone wants that van for a school transport business. Someone else wants to hire that driver for their logistics company. The cold storage manufacturer has other buyers too. The vegetable seller has ample customers at the farmers' market.

So how do you get these resources? You outbid others who want the same resources. If you believe your vegetable delivery will serve customers better than a school transport service, you'll be willing to pay more for that van. Resources naturally flow to wherever they can create the most value, not through some master plan, but through entrepreneurs making calculations about what people need. *(Connect the dots: Turn to page 47.)*

LEARNING FROM THE MARKET

The market is a strict teacher. If people order regularly, they're happy to pay your prices, you can cover your costs and your vegetable delivery service works out, you have created value. The profit you make is the market's way of saying 'Yes, this was needed. Keep going.'

But what if people don't order? Maybe they prefer choosing their own veggies. Maybe your prices are too high. You will lose money, but that loss is also information. The market is teaching you that resources could create more value elsewhere.

Think about successful Indian entrepreneurs. Flipkart's Binny and Sachin Bansal saw that Indians wanted to shop online but did not trust online payments, so they introduced cash on delivery. Paytm's Vijay Shekhar Sharma realized people needed digital payments but did not want complex bank procedures, so he introduced a phone-based wallet. Haldiram's Ganga Bhishen Agarwal transformed the local *namkeen* shop snacks into a packaged-goods empire by acknowledging that people across the country wanted quality and hygiene in their snacks.

Each of these entrepreneurs imagined a future that did not exist yet and also risked investing private capital and their reputation to make it happen.

WHY PERSONAL RISK MATTERS

Entrepreneurs risk private capital, either their own or their family's or in some cases, a venture capital fund's. When it's private money and your market reputation on the line, you become very careful about trying to figure out what people actually want. You talk to customers, you iterate, you adapt.

Compare this with a government official starting a new scheme with government money. If the scheme fails, they don't lose their house or their job. This is not about good or bad intentions, it is about incentives at play. When you have skin in the game, you make different decisions. There's a second problem that's even bigger. Government schemes don't face the test of the market. If people don't use your vegetable-delivery service, you run out of money and shut down. But if people don't use a government bus terminal, it keeps running anyway since it is funded by taxes and not by willing customers. There is no mechanism to redirect those resources to something people actually want.

What emerges from millions of entrepreneurs trying their ideas? A kind of natural selection of businesses. Those who correctly identify what people want and execute well get to expand and get bigger. Those who don't, scale down or eventually shut down. This is how an economy figures out the best ways to serve people's needs. No central planner could possibly know that your neighbourhood needs a pet grooming service but not a photocopy shop. Only entrepreneurs, risking their own resources and learning from customers, can discover this.

The beauty is that when entrepreneurs succeed, we all benefit. We get products and services we value, at prices we're willing to pay, created by people who have to deeply understand our needs to be able to survive in the market.

WHY STARTUPS HAPPEN IN BIG CITIES?

Ever wonder why Bengaluru has more startups than Belgaum? Why does Mumbai produce more entrepreneurs than Madurai? It's not that big city people are smarter or more creative. Big cities are simply better laboratories for entrepreneurship.

Think about it. Want to start that vegetable-delivery service we discussed earlier? In a big city, you'll find many different van dealers to negotiate with (not just one), hundreds of potential drivers looking for work, thousands of busy professionals who might pay for convenience and many cold storage facilities that you can just pay and use. This also means that there might be many more people with the same idea as yours and you face a lot more competition than you'd have faced in a small town or village. As Adam Smith observed, 'the division of labour is limited by the extent of the market.'[4] In simple terms, the more customers you have access to, the more specialized you can afford to be.

In a small town, you might need to run a general store to survive. But in Mumbai, you can run a shop that only sells buttons – and still find enough customers! Someone in Bengaluru can start a business just repairing MacBooks. Try that in a village of 5,000 people!

Cities also create idea collisions. In Bengaluru, a chartered accountant from Chandigarh meets an insurance guy from Jammu. They first meet as representatives of their respective companies but start seeing each other more often over food. One day the chicken they've ordered online for lunch is so bad, it gives them an idea and so Licious is born![5]

These random encounters between people with different skills and problems to solve – that's much rarer in smaller places. This is why cities, despite their traffic and pollution, remain magnets for entrepreneurs. They're not just places with more people – they're places where specialized ideas can find their niche customers, where resources are abundant enough to experiment and where failure doesn't mean starting from zero. Your vegetable delivery might fail, but you've built relationships with suppliers, learned logistics and understood customer behaviour. In a city, you can pivot to meal-kit delivery. In a village, you might just go back to farming.

Internet is changing this equation. Today a graphic designer in Shillong can serve clients in Singapore. A programming teacher in Patna can run courses for students in California. When your market is online, you don't need to be where your customers are. You still need good internet, reliable electricity and access to banking, which cities are better at providing. But increasingly, entrepreneurs can enjoy small-town costs while serving big-city markets. The future might see entrepreneurship spreading beyond just Bengaluru and Mumbai as long as the infrastructure follows.

NEW THINGS SOMETIMES KILL OLD THINGS (AND THAT'S OKAY!)

Akash's uncle ran a public call office (PCO) booth in a small bazaar in Bihar. If you're very young, you might not even know what that is. Through the 1990s and early 2000s, these yellow and black signed shops were everywhere – the only way most Indians could make a phone call. His uncle's shop was always busy. People would queue up, shouting over crackling lines to relatives in Dubai or Delhi, watching nervously as the meter ticked up the rupees. Then mobile phones arrived. First for the rich, then cheaper Chinese models, and suddenly everyone had a phone in their pocket. Akash's uncle saw the writing on the wall. His PCO booth also started offering mobile recharges and then completely transformed itself into a recharge and mobile accessories shop.

Figure 6.2: A PCO booth

Figure 6.3: PCO booths transitioned into recharge shops

For a few years, it worked. People needed scratch recharge cards, Subscriber Identity Module (SIM) cards, and someone to help them figure out how these new gadgets worked. But that did not last long. People started recharging online. He ran out of business and had to shut shop. The story of Akash's uncle and his PCO booth is the story of creative destruction. The same technology that killed his PCO booth business unlocked massive value for society. Instead of walking to a booth and waiting in line, anyone could now call from anywhere. Migrants could hear their children's voices every night, not just on Sundays. With the internet, farmers could check crop prices instantly. Small businesses could coordinate with suppliers without having to travel.

THE SEEN AND THE UNSEEN

The destruction is visible and immediate, but the creation is invisible and takes time. When PCO booths closed, everyone could see the shopkeepers losing their livelihood. What was not visible immediately was the new jobs. Thousands of new jobs in mobile tower installation and maintenance, lakhs of people employed in mobile retail and repair shops. Don't forget the new businesses and entire industries not thought of before were built entirely on mobile connectivity and ubiquity. Ola, Swiggy, PhonePe, even YouTube and the people who depend on these apps for their livelihood.

The mobile revolution did end up killing PCO booth jobs. But in due time, it created far more employment than it destroyed. Try telling that to Akash's uncle when his recharge business started failing. The destruction hit him personally and immediately. The creation happened elsewhere, to other people, over many years.

CAN YOU STOP CREATIVE DESTRUCTION?

It is very tempting to say, 'Let's protect existing jobs by slowing down change.' Some countries try this. They subsidize failing industries, ban new technologies or create regulations that put hurdles in the adoption of new technologies. It is like trying to hold back the tide with your hands.

Imagine if we had 'protected' PCO booths by banning mobile phones. Sure, Akash's uncle would still have his business. But crores of Indians would still be queuing up to make phone calls, families would remain disconnected, millions of jobs in the mobile ecosystem would never exist and the bottom line is, we would all be much poorer as a society.

The harsh truth is that protecting dying industries does not save jobs in the long run. It instead spreads the pain to everyone else. We all pay higher prices, get worse services and miss out on innovations that could improve our lives.

Figure 6.4: Mobile phones have reached every corner

The real challenge isn't stopping creative destruction, it is managing the transition. The faster people are able to transition from dying industries to growing ones, the less painful creative destruction is. New industries need skilled workers and displaced workers need retraining.

Today IT professionals worry about AI taking their jobs. Accountants fear automation. These fears are real, just as Akash's uncle's were. But if history teaches us anything, it's that human creativity finds new ways to

Why Did the Industrial Revolution Start in Britain, Not India or China?

Figure 6.5: Cotton mill in the 1830s, part of the Industrial Revolution

The industrial revolution was humanity's greatest episode of creative destruction – transforming agricultural societies into industrial ones, destroying traditional crafts while creating unprecedented prosperity. But why did it begin in eighteenth-century Britain rather than in India or China, both sophisticated civilizations with rich commercial traditions?

The popular narrative often credits colonialism, suggesting Britain industrialized by exploiting its colonies. But this gets the story backwards. The industrial revolution was already underway before Britain's colonial empire peaked. The real push for innovation came from labour *shortages* that forced entrepreneurs to find ways to do more with fewer workers.

Waves of plagues had wiped out half of Britain's population over the preceding centuries resulting in labour scarcity. Patent laws meant inventors could profit from their ideas. Joint-stock companies meant entrepreneurs could pool capital and share risk.[6] All these factors together gave Britain a cocktail that was quite unique: high wages (incentive to replace workers with machines), cheap coal, and crucially, what economist Joseph Schumpeter called a 'business-respecting civilization.'[7]

India might have had sophisticated textile production, advanced metallurgy and thriving commerce at various points in history. But it lacked the scarce-labour and abundant-energy combination as well as the institutional framework that encouraged risk taking. Colonialism certainly did not help but even without it, the industrial revolution would likely have started in Europe.

Creative destruction needs the right environment. It is not enough to have smart people or even commercial traditions. You need institutions that enable risk taking, a culture that tolerates failure and economic conditions that make new innovations profitable.

create value. The question isn't whether jobs will exist, it's whether we will be ready for the jobs that don't exist yet.

THE GREAT CONVERGENCE: (IN)EQUALITY IN THE AGE OF TECHNOLOGY

A Silicon Valley billionaire in California and a farmer in my village in Bihar are separated by vast oceans of wealth. One flies in private jets;

the other has not boarded a plane yet. In the evening though, they might both be scrolling through the same YouTube videos, chatting on WhatsApp, checking the weather on Google. The billionaire's iPhone 17 Pro Max and the farmer's ₹7,000 Android phone do not have that much difference in their core functionality. One costs 20 times more than the other, but the actual difference is surprisingly small. And if you consider a poor American in this example – he'd also be using an iPhone, so the difference shrinks even further.

This is the paradox of our times. Technology might seem to be making the rich richer. But it simultaneously makes everyone's daily experience more similar than ever before.

Figure 6.6: Paul Graham

THE GROWING GAP

Technology creates unprecedented wealth concentration. As Paul Graham observes, technology amplifies differences in productivity.[8] A great programmer is not just slightly better than an average one, they might now be 10 times or 100 times more productive. A successful app can reach a billion users, while a traditional business might serve thousands.

Figure 6.7: Nithin Kamath

Figure 6.8: Nikhil Kamath

This is why entrepreneurs, Graham notes, are the world's biggest manufacturers of economic inequality.[9] When you create something that millions of people want, technology lets you serve them all. Take Zerodha's Nithin and

Nikhil Kamath. In the old world, even the biggest stockbrokers needed physical offices, paper forms, phone operators. Growing meant hiring proportionally more people.

Zerodha built technology that handles millions of trades daily with just a few hundred employees. The 100th customer costs them almost nothing extra to serve. The millionth customer? Still almost nothing. They added only one engineer during COVID-19 and the tech team went from 30 to 31 – while the trades per day went from 2 to over 12 million.[10] This is the leverage that technology brings. The same code that serves one person can serve 10 million. Traditional brokers with thousands of employees and hundreds of branches got disrupted by a company with better technology and a fraction of the staff.

This 'winner-takes-all' dynamic can be brutal. When customers can switch with a click, why would they choose the fifth-best trading app? In the physical world, the best restaurant in Mumbai can only serve so many people. But the best trading app can capture most of the market. The difference between being #1 and #5 isn't 20 per cent more success – it might be 10 times or 100 times more. Technology doesn't create gentle inequality but massive, exponential gaps.

NOT ALL INEQUALITY IS CREATED EQUAL

Not all inequality comes from productive innovation. A lot comes from 'rent-seeking', using connections, licences and government influence to make money without creating value. When a politically connected businessman gets a mining licence through his contacts rather than competitive auction it is called cronyism. When regulations are written to favour incumbents and block new entrants, the system is being rigged.

But even if we eliminated all corruption and cronyism, we would still have inequality. Why? Because technology fundamentally amplifies human differences. A great teacher can now reach millions through YouTube. A brilliant coder can build an app used globally. A great entrepreneur can scale his company faster than ever before.

THE SHRINKING EXPERIENCE GAP

As we discussed earlier, the actual experience of daily life is converging. On Akash's recent trip to the United States, he visited a friend pursuing PhD at a public university and a few days later, a billionaire's house. A PhD student in the United States would count in the bottom 10–20 per cent of earners in the country. And yet their lives were not so wildly different than what one would have thought. Akash was surprised to see both have Dunkin Donuts for breakfast. Standard inequality measures will tell you that the United States is much more unequal than India. But experientially if you asked anyone their first impulse would be to say that India is more unequal and they are not wrong if you think about it from the perspective of consumption inequality.

But even in India, consider these:

- **Entertainment**: Ambani's kids and you probably watch the same YouTube videos.
- **Communication:** Everyone from CEOs to street vendors uses WhatsApp.
- **Information:** Google, and now Perplexity and ChatGPT are at almost everyone's fingertips.
- **Transportation**: The richest Indian sits in the same traffic (maybe in a better car).
- **Health**: Basic vaccines and antibiotics work the same for everyone.

The rich can buy better versions in many cases – first-class flights instead of economy, iPhone instead of Android and private-hospital facilities instead of government ones. But they can't buy fundamentally different technology. There's no secret 'rich people's internet' with different content. No special Dolo 650 that only wealthy people can afford.

This creates a strange new world. One of falling lifestyle inequality. The gap between having a smartphone and not having one is massive. The gap between having a ₹10,000 phone and a ₹1,50,000 phone? Not a lot. In terms of the basic technologies that shape our daily lives, be it the internet, mobile phones, modern medicine, air travel, we are all living in the same century now.

Income inequality does dramatically change access to high-quality education, healthcare and opportunities. The rich can buy time (hiring a help), security (gated communities) and most importantly, options for their children. And while income inequality might appear to be rising, we will see in the next few paragraphs that picture is far more complicated.

The question for India isn't whether technology will create inequality – it will. The question is whether the inequality we create will be the productive kind (that rewards innovation) or the extractive kind (that rewards connections), and whether we will be able to expand access so everyone can benefit from technology's equalizing power.

MOST OF US STILL BELIEVE IN KIDONOMICS

We first used the term *Kidonomics* in chapter 3. *(Connect the dots: Turn to page 38.)* In this section, we elaborate on the concept. As a child at a birthday party when the cake was being cut, you've definitely complained that someone else's piece was bigger and it was not fair that they got more than you did. You were likely not wrong then. When something is just given to you, equal distribution obviously seems fair. The immediate assumption is that if someone got more, someone else must have gotten less.

Most of us never quite outgrow this thinking. So, what we are calling Kidonomics is the idea that wealth is a fixed pie waiting to be distributed, preferably equally, by some authority. It makes perfect sense when you're a child. In most cases, everything you have, be it toys, clothes or pocket money, has been given to you by adults. If your sibling gets ₹500 for Diwali and you get ₹200, you feel cheated. But when you grow up and still carry this mental model into discussions about the real world, it completely breaks down.

THE FIXED PIE THAT ISN'T FIXED

Figure 6.9 The Fixed Pie Fallacy

Headlines like 'India's billionaires doubled their wealth,' prompt the Kidonomics response: 'While the poor got poorer!' It seems logical. If the rich have more of the pie, everyone else must have less, right? Wrong. Because unlike your mother's Diwali money, wealth in an economy is not distributed; it has to be created. And it can be created unequally without taking anything from anyone else.

Consider what happened when Infosys founders became billionaires. Did they take this wealth from poor programmers? Actually the opposite – they created an entire industry that employs millions. When Deepinder Goyal built Zomato into a massive company, did he steal from restaurant workers? No, he created thousands of delivery jobs that didn't exist before.

As Paul Graham points out, this fixation on distribution versus creation is why we misunderstand inequality. We're still thinking like children waiting for cake, not like adults who understand that someone has to bake the cake first. And some people are much, much better at baking.

WHEN SHOULD WE WORRY?

As we discussed earlier, there is a crucial difference between wealth from creation and wealth from extraction. When someone gets rich by creating monopolies enabled by regulations, getting licences through their connections, extracting rents without adding value to the economy and by inheriting advantages that lock out others; we all should be concerned. That's the bad kind of inequality – the kind that actually is zero-sum, where someone's gain really is someone else's loss. This is crony capitalism, and it deserves all the criticism it gets. But attacking all inequality because some comes from cronyism is like banning all restaurants because some have rats.

Instead of asking: 'Why does he have more than me?'
Ask: 'Am I better off than I was before?'
Instead of saying: 'The gap is growing!'
Ask: 'Are both ends moving up?'
Instead of demanding: 'Distribute it equally!'
Pause and Think: 'Will that mean less gets created?'

Think about your own life. Are you upset that software engineers earn more than you, or are you grateful for the technology they create? Do you resent successful restaurant owners, or are you happy to have dining options? Would you prefer everyone to be equally poor, or unequally prosperous?

THE INEQUALITY WE NEED

Some inequality is not just acceptable, it is necessary. It is the signal that tells young people what skills to acquire. It is the incentive that drives innovation. It's the reward for risk-taking. Remove it entirely, and you are distributing poverty equally, everyone equally stuck. The goal shouldn't be to eliminate inequality, but to ensure that it comes from value creation, not value extraction. As Amartya Sen lays out in his work on capabilities approach, we should strive towards a society where everyone has a genuine opportunity to create value and basic dignity and opportunity are available to all. When we see that the bottom is rising, even if the top is rising faster, we should be okay with the resultant inequality.

Next time you hear that the rich are getting richer, don't reflexively think the poor must be getting poorer. That's Kidonomics. Ask instead: Is new wealth being created? Are ordinary people's lives improving? Is there opportunity for mobility?

Because unlike the cake at a children's party, the economy's cake can grow. And when it does, we can all get bigger pieces, even if some get bigger pieces than others.

EVEN INEQUALITY IS DECREASING! THE WORLD IS GETTING MORE EQUAL

Here's something that might surprise you: while inequality within countries has been rising, inequality between people globally has been falling dramatically. The world is becoming more equal, not less.

The Great Global Convergence

For most of human history, where you were born essentially determined your economic fate. In 1820, the average person in western Europe was about 3–4 times richer than the average person in India or China. By 1950, this gap had exploded to 10–15 times. The rich world had pulled away dramatically from the poor world.

But then something remarkable happened. According to economist Branko Milanović, global inequality peaked around 1980 and has been falling since. The Gini index is the standard measure of inequality. In the Gini index, 0 means perfect equality and 100 means one person has everything. Global income inequality as measured by the Gini index fell from about 69 in 1988 to 60 in 2015. That might not sound like much, but it represents the most rapid reduction in global inequality in human history.[11]

How did this happen? Poor countries started growing faster than the rich ones. The Chinese economy grew at 10 per cent annually for decades.

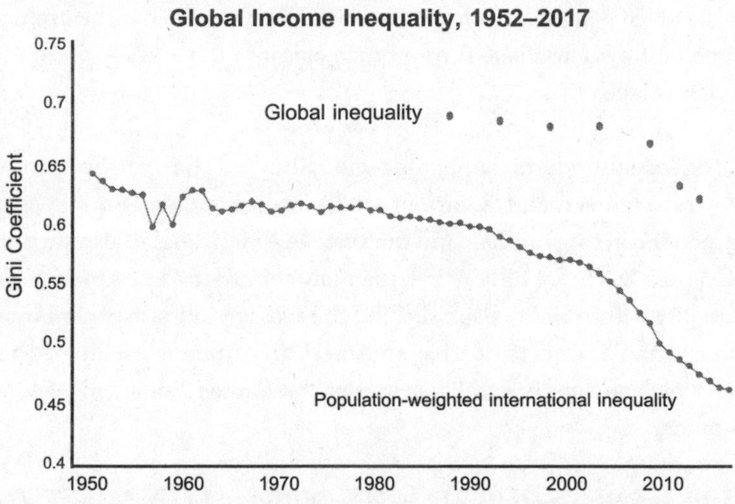

India hit 7–8 per cent. Vietnam, Bangladesh, Ethiopia – country after country began catching up. While an American worker's income might have doubled since 1990, a Chinese worker's income increased 10-fold. An Indian IT worker today earns closer to their American counterpart than ever before. So, why do we always read about rising inequality?

Inequality within countries is rising, while inequality between countries is falling. Both things are true simultaneously.

Think of it this way: imagine two villages, one rich and one poor.

Time Period 1: In the rich village, everyone earns between ₹80,000 and ₹1,30,000 per month. In the poor village, everyone earns between ₹6,000 and ₹8,000. Low inequality within each village, massive inequality between the two villages.

Time Period 2: The poor village develops rapidly. Now people there earn between ₹20,000 and ₹1,00,000. The gap within the poor village has exploded – some earn five times more than others, but the average person in the poor village is now much closer to the average person in the rich village.

This is exactly what's happening globally. Yes, the gap between a software engineer and a farmer in India has grown. But the gap between the average Indian and the average American has also shrunk. China now has more billionaires than any country except America. So inequality within China has risen. But the average Chinese person went from earning 2 per cent of what an American earned to earning 25 per cent, which means inequality between the United States and China has fallen.

THE KUZNETS CURVE: WHY INEQUALITY MIGHT(?) FIX ITSELF

In the 1950s, economist Simon Kuznets noticed something interesting. As countries develop, inequality first increases, then decreases – creating an inverted U-shape.[12]

When economic growth kicks off, some people move from farms to

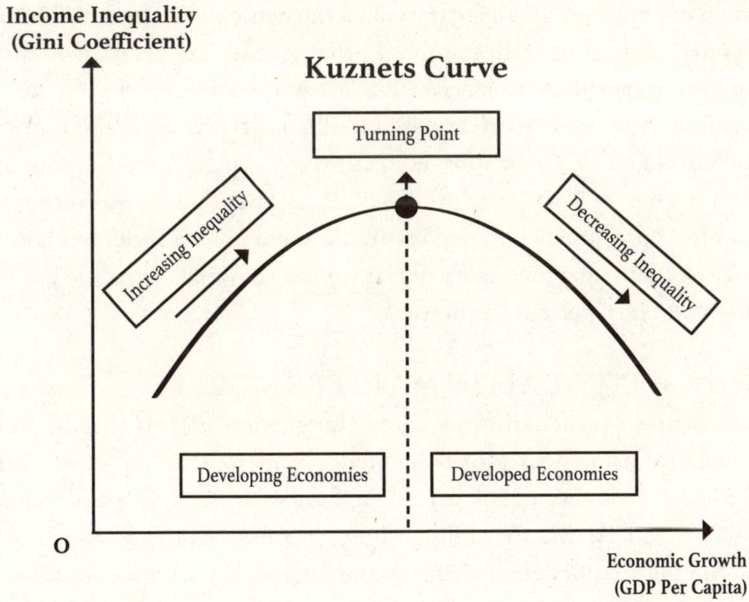

factories first. These early movers earn much more, creating inequality. The farmer still earning ₹10,000 watches his neighbour who moved to the city now earning ₹50,000. Inequality explodes. As growth continues, more and more people make that transition. Education spreads. Workers demand better wages. Government programmes expand. The farmers who move to cities find established networks, better schools and more opportunities. Gradually, inequality starts falling off the high point.

We witnessed this in countries that are considered rich today. Inequality in the United States peaked in the 1920s, fell dramatically through the 1970s, though it has risen again recently thanks to technology. European countries followed similar patterns. South Korea had massive inequality in the 1960s during rapid industrialization but the country is more equal than the United States today.

India might be on the rising part of its Kuznets curve at present. The IT boom, financial liberalization and urban growth are creating winners and losers at different speeds. But if history is any guide, this might not last for long. As more and more Indians get educated and move to the cities and find new jobs, inequality could plateau and eventually, start declining. This is not pre-destined, as Kuznets himself warned. It requires good policies, strong institutions and political will. But it does suggest that rising inequality during a phase of rapid economic growth might not be a permanent destiny.

WHICH INEQUALITY MATTERS MORE?

As discussed earlier, the 'inequality' that matters most is consumption inequality as well as global inequality and by that measure, we're living in the most equal period in human history. From a human welfare perspective, the falling global income inequality deserves to be the bigger story than rising income inequality within countries. It represents hundreds of millions escaping poverty, not just relative poverty but absolute, grinding poverty.

A farmer in Bihar does not resent Bengaluru engineers who earn 50 times more. His own children now have opportunities his generation could not dream of. They can migrate to cities, learn new skills and access global markets. The smartphone in their pocket connects them to the same internet as anyone in New York or London.

This global convergence hasn't concluded yet. India's per capita income is still only about 10 per cent of America's. But that's up from 3 per cent in 1990. If India maintains even 5–6 per cent higher growth than developed countries, the gap will keep shrinking.

The same technology that creates billionaires also enables this convergence. An Indian can learn from MIT professors on YouTube, work for American companies remotely, and sell products globally through Amazon. The barriers that kept poor countries poor for centuries are crumbling.

Yes, some Indians are getting very rich in this process. That's the within-country inequality that makes headlines. What deserves to be the bigger story still is that all Indians are getting richer and catching up with the developed world. Inequality within India will rise, but the question is whether we will continue converging with rich countries, bringing prosperity to hundreds of millions of our people in the process.

Pause and think: Would you rather live in a more equal but poor society or a less equal but rapidly growing one where even the poor are better off?

History suggests you can't have rapid development without some increase in inequality. But history also shows that today's poor countries can catch up faster than ever before. That's the paradox and the promise: inequality everywhere, but a richer, more equal world overall.

Every January, Oxfam releases its inequality report with headlines like '8 men own as much as the bottom 50 per cent of the world !' The media goes wild. Politicians express outrage. But the methodology is so flawed it borders on intellectual dishonesty. Let us dissect the methodology.[13]

1. **The debt trick:** Oxfam measures 'net wealth' – assets minus debts. By this measure, a fresh graduate with an education loan has negative wealth, making them 'poorer' than a subsistence farmer in Bihar who has no debts. That Harvard MBA with $200,000 in student loans? According to Oxfam, she's among the world's poorest people. This is why Oxfam finds more 'poor' people in America and Europe than in China (not in percentages, but even

in actual numbers) – educated young people with mortgages and student loans.

Oxfam and the art of deception

Figure 6.10: Oxfam reports make headlines

2. **Ignoring what actually matters:** While Oxfam obsesses over wealth inequality, global poverty has plummeted. The percentage living in extreme poverty fell from 18.1 per cent to 8.6 per cent between 2008 and 2018. If you look at consumption, what people can actually buy and use, the world is more equal than ever. A poor Indian today has mobile phones, antibiotics and electricity. But Oxfam ignores this because it doesn't generate shocking headlines.
3. **Currency manipulation:** When Oxfam claims the bottom 50 per cent's wealth declined, they conveniently did not adjust for purchasing power or currency fluctuations. If the dollar strengthened that year, when you convert rupees or yuan to dollars, it looks like wealth fell. But could those people buy less food or clothing in their local markets as a result?
4. **Missing Assets:** As economist Hernando de Soto points out, the poor rarely have formal financial assets.[14] Their wealth is in informal

property rights, small businesses and community networks. None of these are counted by Oxfam. A street vendor in an African country might have a thriving business worth millions of dollars, but if it is not in a bank account; Oxfam will count it as zero wealth. Well, he's at least richer than the Harvard MBA according to them!

For an organization that claims fighting poverty as its objective, Oxfam seems oddly uninterested in the greatest poverty reduction in human history. Instead, they stick to sensational statistics intended to grab headlines and donations. Outrage sells, and it sells much better than the story of human welfare.

Next time you see headlines based on Oxfam's annual report, pause and think: Would you rather be a 'wealthy' subsistence farmer with no debt or a 'poor' Harvard MBA with an education loan? Their methodology tells you the farmer is better off. Common sense says otherwise.

THE BOTTOM LINE

This chapter asked two questions that most people think are unrelated. How do some people get rich? And why does that bother us so much? The answers turn out to be connected. People get rich by creating things other people want and technology now lets them serve millions instead of dozens. That same technology also puts a smartphone in a Bihar farmer's pocket that runs the same apps as a Silicon Valley billionaire's. The paradox is that the process that creates inequality is the same process that shrinks it.

The discomfort we feel about inequality is natural. But some of it is also Kidonomics. It is that instinct we have carried from childhood: someone's bigger slice of cake means a smaller one for us. But that happens because we are not thinking of who's even baking that cake.

KEY TAKEAWAYS

- **Innovation** is about finding ways to create more value from existing resources.
- **Competition forces innovation.** Protected markets breed complacency.
- **Entrepreneurs imagine things that do not exist yet** and redirect resources to where they create the most value.
- **Cities are laboratories for entrepreneurship.** They offer denser markets, specialized niches and idea collisions between a much more diverse sets of people.
- **Creative destruction is painful but necessary.** The destruction is visible and immediate; but the creation is invisible and takes time.
- **Protecting dying industries doesn't save jobs in the long run.** It spreads the pain to everyone through higher prices.
- **Technology creates unprecedented wealth concentration**, but it also makes everyone's daily experience more similar than ever.
- **Not all inequality is the same.** Inequality from value creation (innovation) is different from inequality through value extraction (cronyism).
- **Wealth is not a fixed pie.** When someone creates a successful business, the pie grows.
- **Global inequality is decreasing dramatically** as poor countries grow faster than rich ones, even as inequality within countries increases.

- **Rising inequality during rapid development may not be permanent.** The Kuznets curve suggests it peaks and then falls, but only with the right institutions and policies.

7

What Happens When Politics Meets Economics?

Public Choice Theory

♪ Ye jo public hai, kya ye sab janti hai? ♪

What changes about a person when they become a 'public servant'?

The businessman who drives hard bargains, cuts corners and maximizes profit; does he suddenly become a saint when appointed to a government committee? The housewife who haggles over every rupee at the vegetable market – does she stop caring about money when elected as municipal councillor? That software engineer who claims fake rent receipts for tax benefits – does he become scrupulously honest when he joins the income tax department?

We laugh at these questions because the answers are obvious. Yet, somehow, when we think about politics and government, we pretend people transform. We assume

- politicians work for 'public good', not personal gain,
- bureaucrats are motivated by 'service', not salary and promotions,
- voters make choices for 'national interest', not narrow self-interest.

Economics has always been honest about human nature in markets. It puts a lot more emphasis on what people do (revealed preferences) than what people say (stated preferences). Adam Smith's *invisible hand* works because people pursue self-interest.[1]

However, human interactions are not limited to markets alone. Most of our interactions lie outside of market and are non-monetary in nature: when we interact with our family and friends or with our neighbours in residential society and community. There is another kind of interaction which is largely non-monetary and non-market – our interaction with politics and government. When it comes to this, we put on rose-tinted glasses. We somehow expect these people to become saints.

This chapter is about taking off those glasses. It is about applying the same hard-headed logic we use for markets in economics to understand politics. It is about seeing government not as a solution delivered by angels, but as another human institution with all the flaws that implies.

Welcome to Public Choice Theory. It is politics without romance. Public Choice Theory says that 'people are people', whether they are operating in the private market or political market. That they are guided by the same motivations, operating with limited information, and have limited benevolence. These don't change just because people operating in the political market call themselves 'public servants', are working for the 'public good' or 'social welfare'.

By the time you finish this chapter, you'll never look at elections, budgets or government schemes the same way again.

	Private Market Actors: *Consumers, Producers*	**Political Market Actors:** *Voters, Politicians, Bureaucrats*
Motivations	Self-interested	Traditional View: Altruistic Public Choice View: Self-interested
Knowledge	Limited	Traditional View: Unlimited Public Choice View: Limited
Benevolence	Limited	Traditional View: Unlimited Public Choice View: Limited

FRIEDMAN'S LAW OF SPENDING

Nobel laureate economist Milton Friedman explained that there are only four ways in which the money can be spent:[2]

1. Your money on yourself
2. Your money on someone else
3. Someone else's money on you
4. Someone else's money on someone else

Let's make this real with some scenarios:

- **Scenario 1:** You're paying for your own plate at a restaurant. You order one butter chicken, share a *naan* and skip dessert. Bill: ₹500.
- **Scenario 2:** You're treating an acquaintance. You order carefully – enough to look generous, but your wallet is crying. Bill: ₹2,000.
- **Scenario 3:** Your company is paying for a client dinner. Suddenly you discover a taste for prawns and imported wine. Bill: ₹8,000.
- **Scenario 4:** You're a government officer organizing a conference

dinner with ministry funds. *Paneer*? Please. It's five-star catering with 47 items nobody will finish. Bill: ₹5,000 per plate for 500 people.

<table>
<tr><th colspan="4">On whom the money is spent</th></tr>
<tr><td rowspan="4">Whose money is spent</td><td rowspan="2">Yourself</td><th>Yourself</th><th>Someone Else</th></tr>
<tr><td>Strong incentive to economize and seek highest value</td><td>Strong incentive to economize, weaker incentive to seek highest value</td></tr>
<tr><td>Someone Else</td><td>Weak incentive to economize, strong incentive to seek highest value</td><td>Weak incentive to economize and weak incentive to seek highest value</td></tr>
<tr><td colspan="3" align="right">Most government programmes</td></tr>
</table>

Notice the pattern? The further away you get from your own pocket, the more reckless the spending gets. In the first two cases where one is spending their own money either on oneself or on others, there is the greatest incentive to obtain the best bargain for the money spent. It turns out that people don't usually spend someone else's money as carefully as they spend their own. What a surprise, eh!

Of course, love throws a wrench into this neat-looking matrix. You'd likely blow a month's salary on your child's birthday or your parents' medical bill without complaining about it. The closer someone is to your heart, the more their spending starts to resemble your own. Friedman's quadrant works best as relationships start getting more impersonal. Government spending is about as impersonal as it gets.

History and Legacy of Public Choice Economics

Figure 7.1: James Buchanan and Gordon Tullock, Fathers of Public Choice

As far back as the eighteenth century, David Hume and Adam Smith urged us to treat people in government as 'knaves' and criticized the relationship between government and business. But putting it this way, it was blasphemy in the 1960s. Politicians were supposed to be selfless servants of the people! But James Buchanan and Gordon Tullock had the audacity to suggest that the same person who haggles over onions at the *sabzi mandi* doesn't suddenly become Mother Teresa when entering the parliament.[3] For this revolutionary idea that politicians are human, Buchanan won the Nobel Prize in Economic Sciences. Sometimes the most powerful ideas are the most obvious ones.

In India, until recently, the Public Choice Theory was not part of any curriculum in any of the social science departments of our colleges and universities. Study of political decision-making is still not studied in India as carefully as we should. Given the size of the Indian state, and the importance Indians place on elections and politics, the Public Choice Theory has a lot to contribute.

THE PLAYERS AND THEIR GAMES

The Voters: Rational Ignorance

How much time and effort did you spend the last time you bought a mobile phone? If you are like us, it is likely that a decent amount of thought and care went into the decision. Maybe you did some online research, a quick chat with a friend or someone in your family who is tech savvy. You weighed your choices, given your budget, and only then made your choice. It is so because you know that a wrong decision is going to affect you directly.

Think about it. You'll spend hours researching which Diwali sale offers the best TV deal – Amazon or Flipkart? You'll compare EMI options, read 50 reviews, watch unboxing videos. Why? Because you're spending ₹50,000 of your hard-earned money.

But your vote? Whether you vote for Party A or Party B, you still pay the same taxes. The potholes on your street will remain. The government school nearby doesn't suddenly improve. Your one vote among 90 crore voters is like adding one drop to an ocean.

Figure 7.2: Voting in elections

So you do what any rational person would do – you vote based on vibes, WhatsApp forwards or which symbol looks nicer on the ballot. When was the last time you actually read a manifesto? Or checked your Member of Legislative Assembly's (MLA) attendance record? Or even remembered their name six months after voting?

If you answered in the negative to the above questions, it would mean that you were not well-informed when you walked into the polling booth to cast your vote. That you were ignorant while making your choice. Don't feel bad. You're being perfectly rational.

You can guess, and guess right, that the same will be true for almost all voters. In a survey that we have conducted over the last few years with hundreds of college students interested in learning about economics and public policy, on the way to becoming informed citizens, only once have we received an answer in the affirmative. And that person read all the manifestos and got acquainted with all her choices, because it was part of her research project.

What is the probability that your vote will make a difference?[4] Each voter, even though ignorant about sophisticated probability theory, intuitively knows that their one vote is unlikely to change the outcome of the election. It hardly ever happens that a candidate wins or loses an election by just one vote. Voters know that their individual one vote doesn't matter much. All decision-making happens on the margin! And therefore, there is no need to invest much time and energy trying to become an informed voter.

Public Choice Theory teaches us that voters are ignorant when making their electoral choices, but that they are 'rationally ignorant'. This creates a paradox. Democracy depends on informed citizens making thoughtful choices. But democracy also makes it rational for citizens to remain ignorant.

Neta ji's Compulsion

Now let's flip the script. If voters are rationally ignorant, what about the people they're voting for? And the bureaucrats who actually run the government machinery?

Meet *Neta ji*. Before entering politics, he ran a successful transport

business. Tough negotiator, sharp with money, knew how to squeeze every rupee of profit. His drivers still tell stories about how he'd haggle over diesel prices at 5 a.m. Then he joined politics. Suddenly, the same *Neta ji* speaks only of *seva* and *tyaag*. His campaign posters show him as a modern-day saint.

Last month, *Neta ji* inaugurated a new bus stand in his constituency. Cost: ₹15 crores. The same bus stand his transport company would have built for ₹5 crores. But now he's spending government money, not his own. Friedman's fourth law of spending is in action. *Neta ji* is spending other people's money on other people.

Neta ji is still in business, not that of public service but that of vote-maximization. Just like his transport company maximized profits, his political career maximizes votes.

Neta ji isn't evil. He's rational. In business, if you don't make profit, you shut down. In politics, if you don't win elections, you're out. His incentive structure is crystal clear: *Whatever gets votes, gets done. Whatever loses votes, however beneficial for society, gets buried.*

Now you know why every infrastructure project is finished in election year and farm loan waivers are announced just before polls. And why complicated economic reforms that take 10 years to show results are never touched but free electricity that destroys state finances is announced overnight.

Enter the Permanent Government

Politicians come and go. The real power often lies with those who stay, the bureaucrats. The Indian Administrative Service (IAS) officer who's seen seven chief ministers. The section officer who knows where all the files are buried.

Meet Aneesh *ji*. Aneesh *ji* joined as a junior engineer in the Public Works Department (PWD) 20 years ago. Young, idealistic, full of dreams about building world-class infrastructure. Today Aneesh *ji*'s main skill is explaining why things *cannot* be done. 'Rules don't permit this, this one needs committee approval, will have to check the precedent, file has gone to Delhi,' and so on.

Aneesh *ji* is now mature enough to know the basic rule of bureaucracy. He can get in trouble for doing something, but he can't get in trouble for doing nothing. In his transport business, if *Neta ji*'s manager was not performing well, he'd fire him. In government? *Neta ji* can't do that so easily. Aneesh *ji* has seen colleagues who haven't done an honest day's work in decades, yet peacefully retired with full pension and a farewell party.

So, what does Aneesh *ji* want? Not profit; this is not a business. Not votes; he is not elected. What Aneesh *ji* wants is a bigger empire. He wants new schemes, a bigger budget (more importance) and a bigger staff (more people to salute him). Every department needs more budget every year. It is not because bureaucrats want more work, but because they have no incentive (actually a disincentive) to economize. Now, *Neta ji* needs votes. Aneesh *ji* needs budgets. It is a match made in heaven.

Neta ji wants to announce free laptops for a section of students. Aneesh *ji* applauds him on this great idea and puts his requirements forward. He just needs a new nodal agency with 50 private sector contractors and 20 officers, oh and a budget of just ₹1,000 crores. *Neta ji* asks Aneesh *ji* to get a document prepared so that he can present this plan to the cabinet and tells him to move on it fast so that the laptop distribution can happen just in time before the elections. Aneesh *ji* assures *Neta ji* that he is on it and gently recommends that his very 'qualified' nephew is the right person to head the agency. *Neta ji* gets votes from grateful students while Aneesh *ji* gets a bigger bureaucratic empire. And you don't even bat an eye.

A cynic would argue that politics attracts bad people. But that's not true. Many people enter politics with a genuine desire to serve. But the incentives at play convert good people into bad decision-makers. The same *Neta ji* who ran a tight ship in his business now runs a leaky boat in the government. It is not because he forgot his management skills, but because he knows that the leaks are what get him votes. The incentives in our political system are perfectly designed to produce the outcomes we balk at. *(Connect the dots: Turn to page 107.)*

The Business of Influence

In an economy where the state has disproportionate power over markets, business success often depends more on who you know in government than what you know about business. If you want to start a small factory you need government approval to convert the land from 'agricultural' use to 'commercial' use. Getting a power connection will take time and cost you ~12 per cent more than what it does for households.[5] You'll end up paying some 'consulting fee' to a chartered accountant to get a tax registration. Fire safety and environmental clearance permits are so vague that the department official will visit, find faults and 'negotiate'. You need to hire people and that is governed by a plethora of labour laws that sometimes contradict each other. Multiple departments and palms to grease and just as many avenues for harassment. Convoluted rules help established big businesses that can navigate them and regulations become their moat. Elections cost money – lots of it, frankly. Where do the donations come from? What are they buying, if at all?

SMALL GROUPS, BIG POWER

Concentrated Benefits, Dispersed Costs

In 2015, Rapido launched its service. Uber and Ola followed with their own bike taxi offerings. Suddenly, you could zip through traffic for ₹50 instead of paying ₹150 for an auto stuck in the same jam. Tech workers rejoiced. Students could afford daily commutes. Everyone won. Well, everyone except ~1.7 lakh auto drivers.

Let's estimate the maths for Bengaluru:

- An average auto driver loses maybe ~₹250 per day to bike taxi competition.
- An average bike taxi rider saves ~₹75 per day (and a whole lot of time!).
- 1.7 lakh × ₹250 = ₹4.25 crores daily loss for auto drivers.
- 80 lakh × ₹75 = ₹60 crores daily savings for citizens.

	Autorickshaw drivers	Bike taxi users
Number of people	1.7 Lakh	80 Lakh
Daily ₹ at stake	₹4.25 Crore (₹250 x1.7 Lakh)	₹60 Crore ₹75 x80 Lakh)
Meeting points	Auto stands	No natural meeting points
Participation	Enforceable (Union can ban non-participants from stands)	No enforcement mechanism
In case of successful protest	Results accrue to all	Results accrue to all, including non-participants

The citizens' savings are over 14 times higher! So, what happened next?

In July 2021, the Karnataka government issued an order restricting bike taxi services. The platforms fought back in the court but the Karnataka High Court in April 2025 ordered them to cease their bike taxi operations.[6] The Karnataka High Court ordered them to cease operations until the state government frames rules. It was determined that it is the companies' responsibility that the state government hasn't framed the rules.

So, why was there a government push to get bike taxis banned? It was not because they are unsafe (autos have more accidents per km). It was not because customers complained. They could've simply stopped using the services if that was the case. It was because 1.7 lakh organized auto drivers matter more than 80 lakh disorganized Bengalureans who ride bike taxis. Democratic decision-making results in benefits getting concentrated on a few and costs being spread to many.

The pattern repeats in other places:

1. **Farm reforms killed:** A single digit percentage of farmers who benefit from MSP defeated reforms that would've helped most farmers and 100 per cent of consumers.

2. **Wine stays expensive:** ~150 per cent import duty keeps poor-quality domestic producers profitable, taxing crores of urban consumers who are left choosing between overpriced wine and hard liquor. (At the time of writing, India has struck a trade deal with the European Union, under which the tariffs on wine from the EU will eventually go down to ~20–30 per cent.)
3. **Public sector unit (PSU) banks don't get privatized:** Less than 10 lakh employees block reforms that stand to benefit 140 crore taxpayers and citizens.
4. **Foreign direct investment (FDI) in retail blocked:** *Kirana* store associations beat consumers who'd otherwise get access to immense choice in products and save 20–30 per cent on groceries.

Each time, the maths is the same. There is a small group with huge benefits per person, making it worth fighting for. There is a large group with small costs being incurred per person, making it not worth organizing against. The result is that the small minority exploits the majority – very legally and democratically.

Pause and Think: Can you think of a policy in your state where a small group's interests won over what would have been better for everyone?

The Free-Rider Problem

'Bhai, bike taxis are banned! This is middle class harassment! We should protest!'

'Absolutely! You organize, I'll definitely join.' *[Opens Uber, books an autorickshaw.]*

This is you. This is me. This is every educated, tax-paying, rule-following citizen who gets systematically exploited but does nothing. And we're being perfectly rational. Result? Nobody pays. Auto unions win by default. You can tweet but auto unions physically *gherao* the Transport Commissioner's office. Guess who wins?

Why don't bike taxi users have a union? *Simply because the per-person stake is too small to overcome the free-rider problem.*

The free-rider problem gets worse with group size. It's why producer groups beat consumer groups, concentrated interests beat diffused interests, small groups beat large groups and organized minorities beat disorganized majorities. The losers outnumber winners 100:1. But organization beats numbers. Every single time.

At the time of writing, the bike taxi ban has been revoked by the division bench of the High Court of Karnataka in a verdict that overturned the previous single judge order.[7]

So, how did the bike taxi ban go away? It was not the bike taxi users, but the bike taxi drivers who banded together to form The Namma Bike Taxi Association. In a massive show of unity, over 5,000 bike taxi riders from across Karnataka rode to Vidhana Soudha.[8] Now that might have turned some heads!

LICENCE, LOBBY AND LOOT

What is Rent-Seeking?

Meet John and Martin, two brothers who decided to enter the restaurant business in Bengaluru.

John spent ₹2 crores creating the city's best dining experience – imported kitchen equipment, trained chefs and beautiful interiors. His restaurant serves incredible food; customers love it, but he struggles to break even. Why? He could not get a liquor licence. The 'quota was full'.

Martin spent ₹1.5 crores. But not on the restaurant – ₹50 lakhs for a basic set-up, ₹1 crore for leasing a liquor licence from a politician. His food is mediocre; the service is worse. But he's printing money. A beer that costs him ₹100 sells for ₹400.

John created value for his customers by focusing on great food and a delightful experience. Martin just arranged for the liquor licence. In Karnataka, the government has not issued any new licences for retail liquor shops or bars and restaurants serving alcohol since 1992.[9] That does not mean new bars and liquor shops have not opened in Bengaluru. It just means that the liquor licences have become prized possessions and whoever owns them (wink, wink) can sell them in the secondary market for unimaginable multiples.

This is classic rent-seeking. Making money not by creating value, but by manipulating the system to capture artificial scarcity. Each restriction creates 'rent' – the ability to charge more not because you're better, but because competition is illegal.[10] *(Connect the dots: Turn to page 29.)*

Bootleggers and Baptists

For much of the twentieth century in America, an unholy alliance emerged. Baptist preachers wanted liquor stores closed on Sundays for moral reasons. Bootleggers also wanted liquor stores closed on Sundays so that they could make more money by selling liquor illegally on Sunday. They never met, never coordinated, but pushed for the same law. The term was coined by regulatory economist Bruce Yandle when he observed that such alliances were everywhere.[11]

Figure 7.3: Police dumping illegal alcohol (1925), prohibition in California

Take the case of environmental protest against clean nuclear power projects. In the front, you see activists worried about the next Chernobyl even though it has near zero probability. At the back, coal and petroleum lobbies funding the protests.

Environmental groups opposing coastal development are the baptists for the existing resort owners that are afraid of new competition. The result is no new resorts (protecting the environment!), and thus the existing ones are able to charge monopoly prices.

Bootleggers can't say 'ban competition so we make more money'. It is not as much of a winning argument now. So baptists provide them the moral cover under safety, culture, environment, health and social causes that go on. Politicians tend to make the most out of these situations. They can claim the moral high ground by listening to these activists as they are taking action on the pretext of safety, culture, environment, health and blah blah. All this while, they can also get some fat campaign funds from the bootleggers.

When Watchdogs Watch Out for Competition

Post-independence India was suspicious of big business. The 1964 Mahalanobis Committee found that 75 per cent of industrial assets were controlled by just 75 business houses. The top 20 business houses controlled 60 per cent of the private sector.[12] The Parliament thundered with outrage. 'These modern *zamindars* must be controlled!'

In 1969, Indira Gandhi created the Monopolies and Restrictive Trade Practices Commission (MRTPC) to prevent big business houses from crushing competition and exploiting consumers. Any company with assets over ₹20 crores needed MRTPC permission for any expansion.[13] The commission was tasked with ensuring 'fair' competition. Two decades later, these same business houses were still dominant, competition was still dead and consumers were still exploited. How?

Here's what was supposed to happen: big companies would be stopped from expanding, creating space for small entrepreneurs to flourish. Here's what actually happened: Big companies were stopped from expanding. Small companies were stopped from becoming big. And everyone was protected from competition.

Figure 7.4: An old Tata truck

Take Tata's truck manufacturing. In 1975, TELCO (now Tata Motors) wanted to expand production from 24,000 to 36,000 trucks annually. India desperately needed trucks, transporters were paying black market premiums for trucks. The MRTPC said no because they deemed that increasing production will create a monopoly.[14] If you are surprised at that, wait for the real gem. The MRTPC also denied licences to new companies wanting to make trucks because they deemed that the market did not need more producers. So India remained stuck with too few trucks, while TELCO remained stuck at 24,000 trucks and new entrepreneurs remained stuck outside the market. Everyone lost. Except ... the existing players discovered something wonderful. Yes, the MRTPC stopped them from growing. But more importantly, it stopped others from entering. Sure they couldn't expand their cement plants. But the others could not build new ones either. This artificial scarcity meant they could charge monopoly prices for their limited production. The government still had the authority to impose price caps when the prices became politically costly for them.

The watchdog meant to increase competition was reduced to a guard dog keeping competition out, Thus, by the late 1980s, everyone had learned the steps. Big businesses would publicly criticize the MRTPC while privately ensuring that no real competition emerged. The MRTPC publicly restricted big businesses while actually protecting them from competition. The government could claim it was controlling monopolies while collecting donations from the same monopolists.

Everyone won. Except the consumers. Except the people of India. The MRTP Act was finally defanged in 1991 and replaced with the Competition Act in 2002.[15] By then, the country had already lost more than three decades of industrial growth and entrepreneurial energy.

Regulatory capture is not your daylight corruption. It is much harder to detect and punish, and in many cases perfectly legal. This is why it persists.

CAN WE FIX THIS?

After a few thousand words of we showing you how democracy is rigged, how every institution is captured and how you're getting fleeced daily, you might feel like giving up. It is understandable but it is also exactly the wrong lesson.

Remember when you hired that painter to renovate your house while you were away for a wedding? You specifically said 'Asian Paints premium', but returned to find some local brand that'll start peeling in monsoon. You wanted one thing, but the person you hired to do it had different incentives than yours. He pocketed the difference and you got a bad paint job.

Economists call this the principal-agent problem. You're the principal here, the one whose interest is at stake. The painter is your agent as he is acting on your behalf. The problem is that his incentives do not match yours. You want quality, but he wants margin.

Now take this example and scale it up. You're the citizen. The politician and bureaucrat, your painter. You hired them to build roads, maintain law and order, and make good laws on your behalf. But you're away at the wedding; rationally ignorant, busy with your life. The politician and bureaucrat are playing their own games with your money as a result.

How did you eventually fix your painter problem? You probably did one of these three things: hired someone your neighbour recommended and vouched for, stood there and watched the next time, or paid only after inspecting the work. The problem did not solve itself. You had to solve it by changing the incentives of the painter. The same logic applies to the government. The fix does not lie in just finding better people. It lies in building better systems.

Rules over Rulers

Imagine three friends at dinner. Two non-vegetarians, one vegetarian. They vote on where to eat. The vegetarian always loses. Fair? It's democratic! Now scale this up. Two groups can vote to tax the third. It takes only 51 per cent to vote to take from 49 per cent. Or worse, an organized 10 per cent can manipulate the system to exploit the disorganized 90 per cent.

This is why voting in a democracy is not enough. We need a good constitution with rules that put some things as off-limits, no matter who wins the elections. But not all rules are created equal. Compare these two:

1. *The State shall exercise prudence in the management of public finances and avoid expenditure beyond its reasonable means.*

2. *Public debt shall not exceed sixty per centum of gross domestic product. Any breach of this limit shall trigger automatic reductions in government expenditure until compliance is restored.*

Do you see the difference between the two? The first one sounds idealistic but does not mean much. Every finance minister since independence has claimed their budget is fiscal-prudent, all the while running deficits in the same document. The second one on the other hand, is clear, measurable and enforceable.

The best constraints share these few features.[16] They're specific enough that you can tell when they're broken. They trigger consequences automatically rather than depending on someone's judgement. They're hard to change on a whim.

Decisions Closest to the People

The closer a decision is made to the people it affects, the better it tends to be. Your municipal councillor or ward commissioner knows and maybe cares that the *nala* behind your house stinks. The MP in Delhi does not. The secretary in North Block definitely does not.

This is what political thinkers call subsidiarity.[16] Central authority should only do those tasks that cannot be performed well at a more local level. The neighbourhood waste management should not be done by the central government, just as foreign affairs and national defence should not be done by the local government. When decisions are local, decision-makers face greater consequences and citizens can actually influence outcomes. When we allow local governments to compete, moving to another area becomes a check on bad policy and experimentation allows for learning.

Designing for Mere Mortals, Not Saints

So the invisible hand works in markets because competition, property rights and rule of law keep self-interested people in check. What is its equivalent for politics?

Adapt the same ingredients for the political market and we come close to an answer.

1. A constitution that constrains power in the same way competition constrains prices.

2. Separation of powers between the three branches of government: legislature, judiciary and executive. No single branch should be able to capture the system. In India's case, it will also mean a clearer demarcation between the government of the day (executive) and the parliament; and a check on judicial activism.
3. Subsidiarity, so that decision-makers face the discipline of local accountability.

Imagine the horror if the Indian rupee was managed not by the RBI with its clear inflation target of 2–6 per cent but by the bureaucrats at the Ministry of Finance with no measurable mandate at all. Even when the same official moves from the ministry to the RBI, the system around them changes. Clear metrics, public accountability and institutional independence can turn the same human being into a better decision maker. We cannot change human nature but we can change the rules humans operate under.

SO, WHAT SHOULD YOU DO?

Your grandparents had no way of figuring out what their local MP did after getting elected. Today you can look up the attendance records of your MP online. Your parents couldn't coordinate with 500 neighbours to question the ward commissioner. You can do it in a WhatsApp group, even in one that was originally created for Diwali party planning. Earlier you had to be an insider to know where the money went. Today not all but a lot of the budgets, allocations and MP fund spending is trackable. The costs of organizing are falling, and so is the information asymmetry. Public shame on X.com works sometimes. You have more power than any previous generation of citizens. Use it.

Here's the public choice survival guide. When any policy is announced, follow the money. Ask who pays, who gains and who decides. Usually you will see that it is taxpayers who pay, a specific industry or group of people that gains, and a regulator or politician who decides. Check the incentives. Focus on what people do (revealed preferences) than what people say (stated preferences). *(Connect the dots: Turn to page 132.)* Spot if there are any bootleggers and baptists. Whenever you see any strange alliances pushing for the same policy, look deeper. And don't forget Friedman. Nobody spends government money as carefully as their own.

Oh, and if you don't fall under the income tax brackets, don't think you are not a taxpayer. You still are and you are paying for all of this, as most of government revenue in India comes through indirect taxes like GST, which you pay every single time you purchase something.

Once you see these patterns, you cannot unsee them. Public choice is about having this clarity. But it is also about learning to live with some imperfections. You have to come to terms with the fact that concentrated interests will always have an edge over diffused ones. Some degree of capture is inevitable and the system will always be somewhat rigged. But that 'somewhat' matters.

KEY TAKEAWAYS

- **People are people.** Nobody turns into a saint when they get elected or become a bureaucrat.
- **Nobody spends someone else's money as carefully as their own.** Government spending is all about spending someone else's money on someone else.
- **Voters are rationally ignorant.** Politicians are in the business of vote-maximization. Bureaucrats are in the business of maximizing their budgets and turf.
- **Small and organized groups often beat large and disorganized ones.** Concentrated benefits and dispersed costs mean the minority can exploit the majority, legally and democratically.
- **When benefits go to everyone** regardless of who fights, nobody fights.
- **In an economy where rent-seeking has better returns,** the share of productive economic activity declines.
- **Bootleggers and baptists make unbeatable alliances.** Moral arguments provide cover for motives that won't appeal to the public directly.
- **The story of the government is the story of the principal-agent problem.**
- **Decisions should be made closest to the people they'll affect.** The Central authority should only do what local governments cannot.
- **The game might be rigged, but how rigged is what matters.** Understanding it is about designing systems for mere mortals, and not saints.

8 WHO SHOULD DO WHAT?

Parivaar, Samaaj, Sarkaar, Bazaar
♪ Mile sur mera tumhara ♪

Two thousand years ago, a Roman emperor was asked to judge a singing contest. After listening to the first contestant perform, he immediately declared the second contestant the winner.

'But Your Excellency,' his advisor protested, 'you haven't heard the second singer yet.'

'I don't need to,' the emperor replied. 'They couldn't possibly be worse.'

We do this all the time. We assume that the alternative must be better without actually checking. Economists call it the 'nirvana fallacy',[1] and it is the single most common mistake we see people make in policy debates.

Figure 8.1: Roman Emperor

8.2: Band plays at a wedding

But we do not need to go to ancient Rome to see this. You can see it at any Indian wedding. Let us go to a wedding in Delhi. The *pandit ji* is chanting mantras, his voice competing with the band playing '*Gallan goodiyaan*' three tents away. The caterer is frantically plating *paneer tikka* while aunties complain the *dal makhani* is not hot enough.

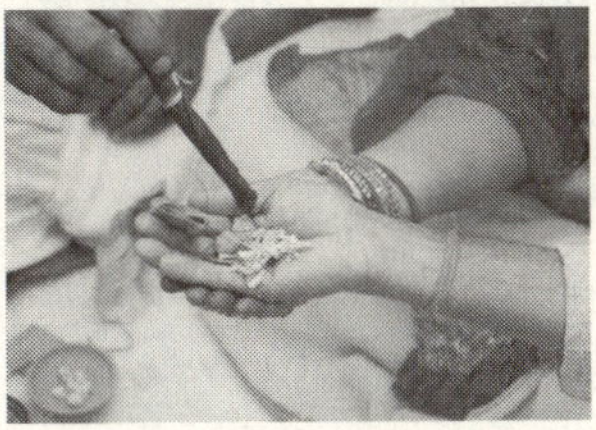

8.3: A wedding ritual

Nobody suggests the *pandit ji* should abandon the *mandap* to check on the kitchen. Nobody expects the band to perform the *pheras*. The caterer is not about to pick up a *dhol*. Everyone knows their rolc.

8.4: Food at a wedding

But zoom out from the *shaadi* and suddenly we are confused. Should the government run airlines? Should markets handle healthcare? Should the caterer also perform the *pheras*? Oh, the last one sounds absurd. But we make equally absurd assignments in our economy every day. We have spent seven chapters understanding how economies work. Now comes the real question: Who should do what?

THE CAST OF CHARACTERS

Every morning, millions of Indians wake up and navigate an intricate dance of relationships, transactions and obligations. Rohini Nilekani puts this in a beautiful framework called *Samaaj, Sarkaar* and *Bazaar*.[2] We add a *Parivaar* to it. So, let's meet our players.

Parivaar, or Family

At 6 a.m. in a middle class home in Indore, Sharma *ji* is making tea while his wife packs meals for their children. Nobody wrote a contract for this. The family runs on an invisible economy of love, duty and habit.

Here, Marx's principle actually works: 'From each according to ability to each according to need.'[3] The earning members provide, the young receive and the old are cared for. It's natural, but only at the level of family. Try scaling it to even a village and you get famines as Mao found out.[4]

Samaaj, or community

Every Sunday in Mayur Vihar, Mrs Iyer coordinates with 15 other families to organize Tamil classes for their children. No one pays her. She doesn't invoice for her time. Yet she shows up, week after week.

This is *samaaj* – the space between family and strangers where people cooperate not for money but for meaning. Your apartment's WhatsApp group organizing a medical camp. College alumni arranging blood donation drives. The local Bengali association celebrating *Durga Puja*.

Human beings are social animals, and they need such cooperation and maybe even validation and recognition from their peers to live a fulfilling life.

Bazaar, or Markets

Walk into any D-Mart at 7 p.m. Thousands of complete strangers cooperating without knowing each other's names, religions or political views. The cashier doesn't care what caste you are.

Remember the double thank-you moments from chapter 2? That's markets – they enable cooperation among people who don't know and might otherwise even hate each other. *(Connect the dots: Turn to pages 16–17.)*

Sarkaar, or State

The last building block of our society is the one that has the least interface with most people – the state, or the government. You may see a police officer once a month or visit a government office once a year, but the state's presence permeates daily life – from the subsidized wheat in your *roti* to the spectrum allocation that enables your Netflix binge. The role of the state varies from country to country. Some countries have a small role for the state, while others have bigger roles in the economic and personal affairs of citizens.

What should be the ideal role of our four characters? To answer this question, let us now turn towards another framework that divides goods and services into four kinds.

FOUR KINDS OF GOODS

Every good or service you use can be sorted into four buckets by asking two simple questions. First: Can I stop you from using it? Your Netflix password? Easy, change it and you're out. The air you breathe? Thankfully not. Economists call this 'excludability'. Second: Does your use reduce what's left for me? You eat that last *gulab jamun*? It's gone. You watch Kapil's show? I can still watch it too. Economists call this 'rivalry'. Now combine these two questions and you get four very different kinds of goods.

Your phone, your backpack, your sandwich; easy to stop others from using, and once you've eaten the sandwich, it's gone. These are *private goods*. Property rights are clear, prices work and markets handle them beautifully.

Now think about the borewell in your colony. It is hard to stop your neighbour from drilling one too, and every litre he pumps depletes everyone's water table. A factory dumping waste into the Yamuna cannot easily be stopped either, and it ruins the river for everyone that lives downstream. These are *common goods*; hard to exclude and easy to deplete. This is where you get the famous 'tragedy of the commons'.[5] (More on that shortly.)

Netflix, your gym membership, or even a toll road; it is easy to keep non-payers out, but your watching Kapil's show does not stop me from watching it too. These are *club goods*. Markets handle them well, as long as someone can control access and charge for it.

Finally, national defence and good law and order. Once provided, you cannot stop anyone from benefiting, and one person's safety does not reduce another's. These are *public goods*. This is where markets struggle.

	I can stop you from using it!	I cannot stop you from using it!
Your use reduces mine	Private Goods	Common Goods
Your use doesn't reduce mine	Club Goods	Public Goods

Now, real life does not stay in neat boxes. Things can shape-shift depending on context.

Think of roads. Empty highways at 3 a.m. are practically a public good. But Bengaluru's Silk Board junction at 8 a.m. is brutally rivalrous. Should we price them differently? Singapore does. If too many people start streaming Netflix at once, your screen starts buffering. My viewing does reduce yours in that case. When it comes to national defence, one could argue that people in Rajasthan's border districts and Jammu & Kashmir have less security available than those in Kerala or Tamil

Nadu. Similarly, people who are more connected, influential and rich have better access to police than those who aren't.

Goods and services are always more or less rivalrous, more or less excludable. The boxes are useful for thinking, not for drawing airtight boundaries.

Pause and Think: What type of goods are education and healthcare?

Case of a Pure Public Good

Here is a thought experiment for you. Can you think of a good that is truly a 'public good', meaning completely non-rival and non-excludable?

Armageddon is a 1998 Hollywood movie in which a large asteroid is found to be on a collision course with earth that will cause global extinction.[6]

NASA comes with a plan to land a spaceship on the asteroid, drill into its surface and detonate a nuclear bomb to break the asteroid into small pieces and change its trajectory. Of course, the mission is successful and the planet is saved.

In this movie world, the service provided by the astronauts who saved the planet is a 'true public good', non-rival and non-excludable for all people inhabiting the earth. No one can be excluded from enjoying the benefit of the service provided by the astronauts, and any one person's benefit (not getting killed by the asteroid) does not reduce the benefit for anyone else.

WHY THIS FRAMEWORK MATTERS

So why even bother sorting goods and services into these four boxes? Because it answers our question of who should do what.

Markets work beautifully for private goods. Your phone, your backpack, your sandwich; the property rights in each of these are clear, prices signal scarcity and competition drives quality. So, why does the Indian government run Hotel Ashok and Hotel Samrat through ITDC? Why does it manufacture condoms through HLL and sell salt through Sambhar Salts? Why does it still run a BSNL,[7] on whose revival Indian taxpayers have spent over ₹3.2 lakh crores (remember Aircel, it closed

Figure 8.5: Hotel Ashok, a government run five-star property

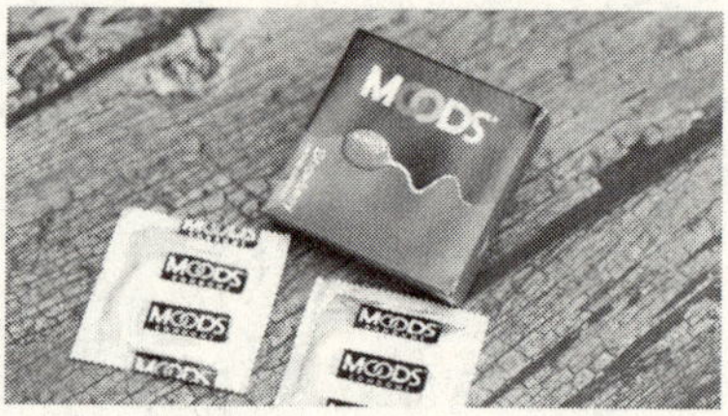

Figure 8.6: Moods condoms, brought to you by the Government of India

down as a result of operating loss of a meagre ₹120 crore). These are goods already being produced by private companies that compete fiercely on everything from price to quality. Every bit of government bandwidth spent on these is bandwidth not spent on courts that have five crore pending cases. Even where the government genuinely wants to help people access a private good; it can just provide the targeted beneficiaries with money in the form of Direct Benefit Transfers (DBTs) and let them buy it.

Figure 8.7: BSNL, taxpayer-subsidized

Markets also excel at club goods.

Netflix, gyms, toll roads, even museums; as long as someone can control access and charge for it, the market handles these brilliantly. But markets struggle with the other two categories.

WHERE *SAMAAJ* OUTSHINES THE *SARKAAR* AND *BAZAAR*

In Keelathenkalam, a village in Tirunelveli district of Tamil Nadu, the smell of *meen kuzhambu* boiling in earthen pots over coal stoves fills every lane on fish harvest day. Families line up at the pond with their pots. Each of them receives a share of fish based on the *vari* (tax) they've paid, not much more than ₹20 per head. Relatives in neighbouring districts get part of this fish harvest as well. This pond is a common good, something we discussed earlier in the chapter. So the standard theory tells us it leads to the tragedy of the commons: overuse, depletion, collapse. But this pond has thrived for generations now!

Each year, the village collects a tax for its temple festival. The leftover money goes to a designated fish harvester, who buys over 45,000 fish eggs at ₹1 each and releases them into the pond after the monsoon recharges the water table. Then the rules kick in. The villagers do not allow any fishing for the next five or six months while the fish grow to four or five kilos each. Everyone knows the rules, follows and enforces them. It is easy to do as the person who might sneak a fish tonight is the person you will see at the temple tomorrow or at the tea stall next week. There is no corporate contract enforcing this or government officials supervising this.[8]

Elinor Ostrom won the 2009 Nobel Prize in Economic Sciences for documenting thousands of such cases worldwide. She studied cases from Swiss alpine meadows and Spanish irrigation systems to Indonesian fisheries and Nepal's community forests. Her discovery upended the widely held consensus that commons inevitably collapse without government regulation or private ownership. She discovered that communities can manage commons effectively, when users know each other, make the rules and weave monitoring into their daily lives.[9] As Ostrom observed: 'There is no reason to believe that bureaucrats and politicians, no matter how well meaning, are better at solving problems than the people on the spot, who have the strongest incentive to get the solution right.'[10] Not so different from Friedman's law of spending, right? *(Connect the dots: Turn to pages 132–133.)*

GURUGRAM'S LESSON IN PUBLIC GOODS

We concluded that markets struggle with providing public goods. So we trust the state to provide these. What happens when it fails?

Figure 8.8 : Gurugram

In *India Grows at Night (2012),* Gurcharan Das provides us with the case study of a fascinating natural experiment.[11] In 1979, Gurgaon (now Gurugram) and Faridabad were split as districts. At the time, Faridabad had an active municipal government, a railway line to the national capital Delhi and a host of industries. Gurgaon, on the other hand, was a rocky farmland. It had no local government, no rail link and no industries. Three decades later, Faridabad had stagnated while Gurgaon had become the 'Millennium City'. It had offices of gleaming towers housing IT parks and Fortune 500 companies, numerous malls and golf courses and some of the most expensive housing developments in all of India. What led to this?

Gurgaon was classified as multiple different villages up until 2008. With no municipal body, there was less red tape and fewer bureaucrats blocking development. Haryana chief minister's office controlled land permissions through a single window, enabling private developers like DLF to assemble vast parcels of land and build residences, office parks and commercial complexes at a breathtaking speed. After liberalization, Gurgaon soared alongside the IT boom. Gurgaon grew from 121,000 people in 1991 to 1.5 million by 2011.

Economists Shruti Rajagopalan and Alex Tabarrok note that DLF set up its own sewage treatment plants, water systems, power backup and even India's first private fire station; with 90-metre hydraulic platforms that outperformed anything the Mumbai government owned. A DLF fire official put it bluntly: 'The government equipment is a joke. They are using a *pichkari* to fight fires in high-rise buildings.' Private security guards in Gurgaon outnumber public police 11:1 and private electricity capacity exceeds public capacity. But the private developers built within their property lines. So that leaves the city with the absence of a functional citywide sewage system, untreated waste dumped on common land, arterial roads without traffic lights and no mass transit connecting the islands. They observe that the private sector has converted public goods into club goods in Gurgaon, but the genuinely public goods that could not be gated, rotted. Compare this to Jamshedpur, a city built by Tata Steel over a century ago. Since Tata as a company had an encompassing interest in the whole city, it built infrastructure that served everyone. Jamshedpur has consistently had some of the highest power availability in India, drinkable tap water, 100 per cent sewage treatment and ranks among India's best-governed cities.[12]

Gurgaon's lesson outlines how markets provide public goods *up to the property line*. Beyond that, you either need a state focused on providing public goods, or a single private entity with encompassing interest, like

Tata in Jamshedpur. As Gurcharan Das wrote in 2012, India grows at night when the government sleeps, but the missed opportunity is that India also needs to grow during the day.

So far we have been asking who should provide which goods. But even with private goods, where markets work best, price signals can sometimes go wrong.

Figure 8.9: Sir Dorabji Tata Park, Jamshedpur

EXTERNALITIES

In November, Delhi's air quality index (AQI) hits numbers that break the scales. It gets so bad that 'severe' does not even capture it. Those out in the streets feel it in their throats and tourists wear N95 masks even for selfies at India Gate, which appears hazy in the pictures thanks to the thick blanket of smog.

In Gurgaon's DLF Phase 3, Mr Maurya seals his windows and runs big air purifiers. His monthly electricity bill has doubled, his son's asthma medication costs ₹3,000 and his wife has not been able to take her morning walk in months. The trucks thundering down NH-8 and the farmers burning stubble after harvesting their produce in Punjab did not include Mr Maurya's family in their cost calculations. The market transactions they undertook were blind to the cost paid in lungs and lives by countless families like Mr Maurya's. This is a negative externality; costs imposed on people who were not part of the transaction. The price of diesel does not include Mr. Maurya's son's inhaler.

When Miss Rao plants a garden on her South Delhi terrace, her neighbours get (slightly) cleaner air, (slightly) cooler temperatures and property values and rental yields rise a bit. She pays for the plants but her neighbours get some benefits for free as a result. This is a positive externality; benefits accruing to people who were not part of the transaction.

Externalities mean that the market price is not accounting for everything. It is either too low as a result of costs being dumped on others or too high as a result of benefits leaking out to others. Economists have thought about these questions.

Pause and Think: What externalities are patents and intellectual property laws trying to solve for and how?

Ronald Coase: 'Define Property Rights'[13]

Two neighbours in Vasant Kunj. One runs *tabla* classes (noise), the other needs quiet for online meetings. Ronald Coase said: 'Let them negotiate.' Maybe the musician pays for soundproofing, maybe the professional pays for different timing. As long as they can talk and transaction costs are low, they'll find the efficient solution, you do not really need the government. Define who has the right, then let the parties bargain. Coase was awarded the 1991 Nobel prize in Economic Sciences for this insight.

But try this with hundreds of thousands of cars and millions of lungs in Delhi. Coase, however, would not give up. Economist Shruti

Rajagopalan writes that if Coase could advise the Delhi government, he would persuade the chief minister to simply pay farmers in Punjab and Haryana to stop burning stubble.[14]

Figure 8.10: Stubble burning in Punjab

Carbon markets draw from a similar Coasean insight. They create property rights in the externality itself and let the markets work from there. An Indian start-up removes carbon from the atmosphere at a Darjeeling tea estate and sells the credits to a Japanese automobile major looking to offset its emissions.[15] The tea estate gets a new revenue stream, the car company meets its climate commitments, and the atmosphere has less CO_2.

Arthur Pigou: 'Price the Externality'[16]

What if negotiation is not very practical? There are too many parties or just the complexity is too high. Arthur Pigou said: Just use prices. Tax activities that create harm subsidize those that create benefit. Make the price tag closer to what it'd have been if it could account for the externalities.

Consider Bengaluru's traffic. If you have ever got stuck on Outer Ring Road at 6 p.m. on a weekday, you know the problem. Every car entering the road during rush hour imposes a cost in terms of slower speeds, wasted fuel, lost time and worse air quality. But the car owners do not pay for it. Their cost is just their fuel (and maintenance). The cost to everyone else is invisible today. A Pigouvian solution would make that cost visible. Charge a congestion fee that's higher during peak hours and lower at off-peak times. Singapore and London, among other cities have done this very successfully. Bengaluru has debated it for years and yet it has not happened, partly because of political resistance (which party wants to seem to be charging people to drive?), partly because of implementation challenges and partly because the costs of congestion are dispersed across millions of commuters while the costs of the solution fall firmly on a slightly more identifiable group of car owners and riders.

Command and Control

When negotiation is impractical and pricing politically difficult, governments often reach for the bluntest tool: command and control. Instead of taxing pollution, the government mandates cleaner engines. Instead of pricing congestion, it does odd-even schemes. The problem with this approach is that it discourages any innovation. Prices give people room to innovate while mandates tell them exactly what to do.

MARKET POWER

In 2007, the famous business magazine *Forbes* ran a cover arguing that Nokia with one billion customers across the world was so far ahead that

Figure 8.11: Monopolies that weren't?

it'd be difficult for anyone to 'catch the cell phone king'.[17] Four years later, Nokia was gasping for survival.

A decade earlier, in 1998, another famous business magazine *Fortune* ran a story explaining how Yahoo! had won the search wars.[18] This spectacular misreading of market power happens constantly. We see a dominant company and assume their position is permanent. We confuse market share with market power.

What we forget to ask is: dominant over what exactly?

Consider Indian Railways. It is a textbook monopoly as it runs every train in India. But when your cousin needed to travel from Mumbai to Delhi last month, she compared the Rajdhani Express (₹2,200, 16 hours) not to another train but to an IndiGo flight (₹3,500, 2 hours) and even her own car (₹7,500 in petrol, 24 hours). Indian Railways might be monopolizing trains but it still competes in domestic long-haul transportation. This is why market definition matters. Define the market narrowly enough, and everyone's a monopolist. Your corner *chai tapri* has a 'monopoly' on *chai* and biscuit at midnight within 100 meters. Define it broadly enough, and nobody is.

Pause and Think: How does Amazon's or Flipkart's market power fare? Whom do you compare these platforms with when you make a purchase decision?

There are cases where network effects create market power. Take Meta. WhatsApp has market power because your grandmother uses it, and so does your cool cousin and friends. Its value increases with each user. But even this proves fragile. Ask Orkut. Network effects create market power, but only until a better network appears.

Try laying your own tracks to compete with Indian Railways. That's an

Figure 8.12: Coal mining

extreme example. There are countless industries where private parties can operate but need onerous licences and permits, and sometimes must purchase rights to a block from the government (coal mines, for example). The more onerous the regulations, the wider the moat; and the moat was dug not by the company but by the government. Genuine market power which is the ability to raise prices without losing customers comes primarily from government protection.

INFORMATION ASYMMETRY

Sunday afternoon, Karol Bagh used car market. You're examining a silver Maruti Swift – 2019 model and 40,000 kilometres on the odometer. The seller, Mr Verma, knows the engine needs work within six months. He knows the AC compressor is dying. He knows why he's really selling. What do you know at the time? You know that the car is ... silver. This knowledge gap, where one party knows critical information the other does not, can poison entire markets. George Akerlof won a Nobel Prize for explaining why.[19] But markets also evolve ingenious solutions to deal with this asymmetry.

Figure 8.13: Maruti Swift

Platforms as Mediators

Year 2006, Kolkata. Akash's dad took him to a restaurant near Park Street that promised 'authentic Bengali cuisine'. The *baingan kasundi* arrived swimming in oil, the *rosogolla* tasted like sugar-soaked rubber. They paid, left hungry and had no way to warn the next victims.

Today that restaurant would be dead in six months with photos of that oil slick on Google reviews, coupled with brutal Zomato and Swiggy reviews. This is not just word-of-mouth getting digitized. Platforms created enforcement mechanisms that never existed before. Remember that Maruti Swift? Maruti itself started something called True Value to solve this problem.

Certifications as Signals

Remember Rajesh Anna's garment factory in Tiruppur from the second chapter. He still exports cotton garments abroad. His factory has three certificates prominently displayed: WRAP (workplace safety), OEKO-TEX (chemical safety) and SA8000 (labour standards). These are not government requirements. Walmart demanded them.[20].

Rajesh Anna cannot fake this signal, the cost of Walmart debarring his factory would destroy his business. That expense separates serious exporters like him from fly-by-night operators. For Walmart, it also makes things easy as they do not need to inspect thousands of suppliers. They just check for certificates that are not possible to fake. *(Connect the dots: Turn to pages 29–30.)*

But the government sees these market certifications and thinks: 'We should do it ourselves. It will help the consumer.' ISI mark started as quality assurance. Now it is mandatory for over 450 products.[21] What began as information became permission.

Brands as Trust Proxies

Even in 2006 Kolkata, Akash's dad had an escape route from restaurant roulette. An Oh! Calcutta or Peter Cat outlet at the Forum Mall in Bhawanipur. It would have been more expensive but the brand premium would have served as information insurance. That extra ₹200 per plate bought the knowledge that someone, somewhere, had standards to maintain.

He could have also just taken me to McDonald's that had just opened on Park Street. The McVeggie there would have tasted just like the one in Mumbai, or even Minnesota. It wouldn't have been the best food we had ever eaten but it would not have been surprisingly terrible. Chains like McDonald's offer a kind of predictable mediocrity which can be worth billions. It is because one franchise serving spoiled patty in Kolkata could damage McDonald's nationally, and maybe even globally. So they have a stronger incentive to control supply chains and enforce standards.

Brands solve information asymmetry by putting reputation on the line. But what happens when stigma prevents the natural reputation mechanism of the market from working? Consider men's sexual health. If you've ever taken a train through the hinterlands, you would have seen walls plastered with quacks guaranteeing '100 per cent results'. One in four men experience a sexual health issue, and most are treatable but stigma prevents people from talking, and when people don't talk, information markets collapse. Akash's start-up, Raaz MD, is trying to build a trusted brand in this broken market, combining AI-powered assessments paired with verified doctors, generating reports the patient can actually read, understand and question.

Artificial Intelligence and Information Asymmetry

Platforms, certifications and brands have all chipped away at information gaps in the last century. But they barely touch the most expensive decisions we make.

Figure 8.14: Medical diagnosis

Take medical diagnosis. You visit three doctors for chronic back pain. The orthopaedic surgeon recommends a spinal fusion surgery that would cost ₹3 lakhs. The physiotherapist says you don't need that, and six months of therapy would do for just ₹50,000. The third doctor prescribes longer rest and painkillers, costing you just ₹500.

Who is right here? You have no way to know that. This is not like that bad restaurant where you taste the food and leave a Zomato review. Even after treatment, you cannot verify the quality. If surgery works, you'd still be asking yourself if it were necessary, or would rest and therapy have done the job? If it fails, was it the surgeon's skill or just your bad luck?

Now imagine this. You're in the surgeon's office. He recommends spinal fusion. You point your phone at your MRI scan. Within minutes, artificial intelligence (AI) analyses it against thousands of similar cases. It has compared success rates for surgery versus physiotherapy for your particular condition. It has checked this surgeon's outcomes against city averages and flagged any inconsistencies in the diagnosis. You are no longer just trusting one doctor's word. You have a second opinion at your fingertips.

This is not science fiction. AI already reads certain X-rays more accurately than radiologists and detects skin cancers that dermatologists miss.[22] Technology is collapsing information asymmetry in fields where it was once considered permanent. When AI gives the buyer even limited access to the same pattern recognition that took the seller decades to acquire, the market failure gets solved partially.

WHEN SHOULD THE STATE INTERVENE?

> 'The difference between successful people and really successful people is that really successful people say no to almost everything.'[23]
>
> **– Warren Buffett**

For his new year's resolution this year, Rudra decided to meditate every morning, go to the gym daily, master Spanish, read 50 books, cook healthy meals and launch a side business. By week three, he was eating instant noodles, had practised his Spanish lessons just twice, and the meditation app he had installed was already off-loaded by the app store to save space. Sounds familiar?

This is not a willpower problem. It is a bandwidth problem. Even with the full authority to reorganize his life, Rudra lacks the capacity to sustain multiple new habits simultaneously. One or two changes could have been possible but not six at a time. Now scale this up. If individuals with complete autonomy over 16 waking hours can't do everything, how can we expect governments managing millions of people to excel at everything?

Companies discovered this decades ago. General Electric (GE) once made everything from light bulbs to jet engines to financial services. Jack Welch recognized the problem and famously declared they'd be 'number one or two in every market or get out.' Even GE, with vast resources, couldn't excel at everything simultaneously.[24] Today's most successful companies focus on core competencies ruthlessly. Apple's product range is still countable on fingers.

If this constraint binds individuals with full control over their time and companies with billions in resources, it must bind governments too. Yet we routinely expect the state to do everything and thus you get the government equivalent of Rudra's failed January resolutions. We have already discussed that the government in India produces private goods; hotels, condoms, salt, even a telecom operator. The problem runs far deeper than that though. The government also sells beer (Tamil Nadu and Kerala) and manages coal mines. Meanwhile, police stations lack basic investigation equipment and courts have five crore pending cases.

This is a classic bandwidth problem. Think of state capacity like random-access memory (RAM) on your computer. Run four programmes and each gets enough memory, so everything works. You run 20 at a time and everything slows to a crawl.

India as a Flailing State

Development economist Lant Pritchett captured this perfectly with his term 'flailing state' – not failing, but flailing.[25] Like someone drowning who can still wave their arms but can't swim to shore.

India, Pritchett notes, can put a spacecraft on Mars but can't ensure teachers show up to village schools. It's not that India lacks capability – Mangalyaan proves otherwise. It's that spreading limited capacity across unlimited ambitions leaves no bandwidth for basic functions.

His research documents the gap between state authority (what the government can legally do) and state capacity (what it can actually accomplish). India has the authority to run everything from space programmes to neighbourhood schools. But when Pritchett studied the actual implementation, he found that 48 per cent of government teachers were absent during random checks, and 69 per cent of those who paid bribes for driver's licences couldn't actually drive safely.

Strategic Subtraction as a Solution

Limited bandwidth plus unlimited ambitions equals universal mediocrity. Just as Rudra eventually succeeded by focusing on one habit at a time, governments must strategically subtract rather than continuously add responsibilities. Every non-essential function the government abandons frees capacity for core responsibilities: law and order, justice, basic infrastructure.

SO, WHO SHOULD DO WHAT?

Remember that wedding in Delhi from the beginning of the chapter? The caterer was frantically plating *paneer tikka* when someone suggested he also perform the ceremony. Everyone laughed because it was so obviously absurd, and yet we are fine with our government manufacturing condoms while urban infrastructure crumbles.

Markets excel while delivering private goods and club goods. Your local *chai tapri* opens late because profit motivates service. Innovation takes place regularly in markets because someone can get rich solving your problem. When people are able to choose and pay individually, markets deliver miracles.

Communities thrive while managing common goods. That Tamil Nadu village pond flourished because everyone knew everyone. Local tribes can manage their forest land much better than the forest department.

Governments should be duty bound to provide us public goods well, first and foremost. One cannot buy one's own slice of national defence. But in cases of market failure, we commit the mistake the Roman emperor did far too often. Instead of asking the government to step in every time there is an 'apparent' market failure, we should first ask if that would make it worse?

A POLICY MANTRA FOR YOU

Next time you are debating a policy, be it in an argument at your local *chai tapri*, on WhatsApp groups or on a news channel; run it through three questions.

First, what kind of good is this? Is it a private good, a club good, a common resource or a public good? The answer should tell you who should be in charge. If your impulse for a private or common good is also that more people should have access to it, consider whether a philanthropy or the government can just subsidize it for certain sections instead of producing it.

Second, who is paying, who is gaining, and who is deciding? Follow the money, just as we learned in chapter 7. If the costs are going to be spread thin across crores of people while the benefits are going to be concentrated on a few, you are almost certainly looking at a small group capturing the system.

Third, what is the counterfactual? Don't be the Roman emperor. Don't just assume the alternative is automatically better. If the market is failing, ask if a bad regulation is behind that failure. Often a bad government policy also causes market failure. Even if that is not the case, ask whether the government has the bandwidth, the information and the incentives to do better. As the famous aphorism goes, *perfect is the enemy of good.* It is not always useful to ask if a solution is perfect. But it is always useful to ask *'compared to what?'*

These three questions are not enough to give you all the answers. But along with everything we learned in this book, they are good enough to inoculate you against the most common mistakes people make while thinking about policy.

KEY TAKEAWAYS

- **Every society runs on four players:** family (*parivaar*), community (*samaaj*), markets (*bazaar*) and government (*sarkaar*).
- **Every good or service can be classified by two questions:** can people be excluded from using it, and does one person's use reduce what's left for others? The answers determine who among the players should provide it.
- **Markets handle private goods and club goods beautifully.** The government should have no business producing goods the market already provides well.
- **Commons don't always collapse.** Communities have demonstrated that they manage shared resources effectively.

- **The government's first and foremost** function should be providing public goods.

- **The Nirvana Fallacy** is the most common mistake people make in policy debates. Before asking the government to fix a market failure, ask if there is a possibility of the government making it worse. Don't compare imperfect markets to an imagined perfect government.

- **Externalities are real, but the solutions are wide ranging.** Start with defining property rights (Coase) or pricing the externality (Pigou).

- **Market power is temporary, but government regulation can make it permanent.** Don't confuse market share with market power.

- **Information asymmetry has market solutions that keep evolving** – brand, platforms, certifications and brace for artificial intelligence.

- **State capacity is finite.** Every non-essential function the government takes on is bandwidth stolen from its core function, which is provision of public goods. Strategic subtraction, and not continuous addition, is the path to building a capable state.

EPILOGUE

FROM SCARCITY TO ABUNDANCE AND BACK TO YOU

We began this book in Akbar's palace. The Shahenshah-e-Hind was suffering a toothache with no remedy but cloves and prayers. He had 40 dishes served for lunch but no tomato, no potato and no chillies. He could call musicians on demand, but only the ones that were already in the palace. He had to wait for two weeks to send an urgent message to Bengal and two more weeks to get a response.

And then we asked you to picture yourself. You are likely lying in bed, with your AC at 24°C and any song you want to listen to at your finger tips. You are chatting with a friend across the country – or for that matter, even globe – and making up your mind between pizza, Thai curry and a protein bowl to have for food. We're not sure if you had ever thought that your life would have made even an emperor like Akbar jealous.

How did we get here? Eight chapters later, you should have the answer. Not that it is one single answer, but you have a web of interconnected ideas that can help you with one.

We got here because people trade. A Chilean lithium miner and a Noida factory worker and a salesman from Vijay Sales can cooperate with each other without ever meeting. We are each doing what we do best and we trade for the rest. The number of double thank-you moments that make both sides better off are exponentially higher in today's world than in Akbar's.

We got here because prices talk. A spike in onion prices whispers to a Nashik farmer to plant more and a drop in tomato prices tells a Bengaluru restaurateur to update his menu with more Arrabbiata recipes. These signals coordinate billions of decisions every moment, with no master planner in charge.

We got here because money, when it holds its value, works as the nervous system of this coordination. And when it does not, when governments attempt to print their way to prosperity, we get inflation, an invisible tax that robs us of our savings and poisons the signals that made the coordination possible.

We got here because some societies built institutions that rewarded creation over extraction. But remember that the prevalent ideas in those societies changed, and the rules followed.

We got here because entrepreneurs imagined things that did not exist and risked money to make them happen. Creative destruction, painful as it is for those who bear its immediate cost, replaced the PCO booth with the smartphone and bullock carts with cars and tractors.

We got here despite politics, not because of it. Concentrated interests have always captured policy, voters have always been rationally ignorant and much of government spending has always been wasteful. But the degree of it all matters.

And we got here because, even if imperfectly, we learned what institutions are best for which tasks. We have not always got the assignments right but the broad direction of progress has been one of letting markets trade, communities govern their commons and the state focus on what only it can provide. Prosperity has ensued when we have followed this insight and we have stumbled when we have forgotten it.

The story of economics is the story of humankind's long walk from scarcity to abundance. That walk was not guaranteed. Bad ideas can still reverse it. Countries that were once rich have stagnated. Societies that once had open markets have walled them off. Civilizations that trusted commerce have tried to replace prices with planners, and paid the price for it.

What keeps the walk going is ideas. As Keynes wrote, the world is ruled by little else. The ideas in this book are not mere academic propositions. They are the engines of modern prosperity we enjoy today. You now carry these ideas with you. You now see what was hitherto unseen.

The promise of this book was to equip you with a lens to see the world with. The lens of economic thinking helps you look not merely at the immediate, but at the longer-term effects; not merely at the consequences for one group, but for society at large. India needs more people who can think clearly about trade-offs. We need more people who can resist the seduction of simple stories and ask the right questions.

We wrote this book because we believe that these ideas have the power to change how India thinks about its own future. The change would not have come through a grand revolution, but through a change in ideas we believe in as a society. It would come when in your *chai tapri* arguments, and even in the quiet moments when you read a headline, you pause to ask: 'But what about the unseen?' That is all economics really is. It is the art of seeing what most miss.

Now go see.

REFERENCES AND RECOMMENDATIONS

CHAPTER 1: WHAT IS ECONOMICS, REALLY?

1. Rosling, Hans, Ola Rosling, and Anna Rosling Rönnlund. *Factfulness: Ten Reasons We're Wrong About the World – and Why Things Are Better Than You Think*. New York: Flatiron Books, 2018.
2. Bylund, Per (@perbylund), "What causes #poverty? Nothing. It's the original state, the default and starting point. The real question is, What causes #prosperity?" X (formerly Twitter), Nov 15, 2015, https://x.com/PerBylund/status/665900726388785153.
3. Marginal Revolution University. "The Hockey Stick of Human Prosperity," June 25, 2014. https://www.youtube.com/watch?v=t9FSnvtcEbg.
4. Bastiat, Frédéric. "That Which Is Seen, and That Which Is Not Seen." 1850. In Selected Essays on Political Economy, translated by Seymour Cain, edited by George B. de Huszar. Irvington-on-Hudson, NY: Foundation for Economic Education, 1995.
5. Hazlitt, Henry. *Economics in One Lesson: The Shortest and Surest Way to Understand Basic Economics*. New York: Harper & Brothers, 1946.
6. Hayek, F. A. "The Use of Knowledge in Society." *The American Economic Review* 35, no. 4 (1945): 519–30. http://www.jstor.org/stable/1809376.
7. Harford, Tim. *Fifty Things That Made the Modern Economy*. London: Little, Brown, 2017.
8. Keynes, John Maynard. *The General Theory of Employment, Interest and Money*. London: Macmillan, 1936.

CHAPTER 2: WHY DOING EVERYTHING BY YOURSELF IS A TERRIBLE IDEA?

1. Read, Leonard E. "I, Pencil: My Family Tree." The *Freeman*, December 1958.
2. Norberg, Johan. *The Capitalist Manifesto: Why the Global Free Market Will Save the World*. London: Atlantic Books, 2023.
3. Jacobs, A.J. *Thanks A Thousand: A Gratitude Journey*. New York: Simon & Schuster/TED Books, 2018.
4. Stossel, John. "The Double 'Thank You' Moment." ABC News, May 31, 2007. https://abcnews.go.com/2020/story?id=3231572.
5. Smith, Adam. *An Inquiry into the Nature and Causes of the Wealth of Nations*. London: W. Strahan and T. Cadell, 1776.
6. Ricardo, David. *On The Principles of Political Economy and Taxation*, 1817.
7. Centre for Civil Society. "The Fate of a Second-hand Premier Padmini: Mohit Satyanand," March 29, 2016. https://www.youtube.com/watch?v=rM5QO4lKCOs.
8. George, Henry. *Protection or Free Trade*, 1886.
9. Reed, Lawrence W. "The Man Behind the Hong Kong Miracle." Foundation for Economic Education, February 10, 2014. https://fee.org/articles/the-man-behind-the-hong-kong-miracle/.
10. Badri, Shruthi (@shruthibadri), "in light of recent events i started looking into the manufacturers of my favorite clothing brands and kept running into a common pattern...why did they all manufacture in pakistan, china, turkey but not india?" X (formerly Twitter), May 9, 2025, https://x.com/shruthibadri/status/1920549796919849002.
11. Ministry of Finance, Government of India. "Recommendations of the 56th Meeting of the GST Council held at New Delhi, today."

Press Information Bureau, September 3, 2025. https://www.pib.gov.in/PressReleasePage.aspx?PRID=2163555

CHAPTER 3: WHAT ARE PRICES TRYING TO TELL YOU?

1. McCloskey, Deirdre Nansen. "The Labor Theory Is Wrong." *Deirdre Nansen McCloskey* (blog), April 15, 2024. https://mccloskey.substack.com/p/the-labor-theory-is-wrong.
2. Smith, Adam. *An Inquiry into the Nature and Causes of the Wealth of Nations*. London: W. Strahan and T. Cadell, 1776.
3. The Fraser Institute. "Essential Coase: What Are Transaction Costs?," July 30, 2021. https://www.youtube.com/watch?v=JsQ7tc3G-KQ.
4. Marginal Revolution University. "Opportunity Cost and Tradeoffs," August 23, 2023. https://www.youtube.com/watch?v=uorrlWJ23Mg.
5. Jevons, Marshall. *Murder at the Margin: A Henry Spearman Mystery*. Glen Ridge, NJ: Thomas Horton and Daughters, 1978.
6. Marginal Revolution University, "The Equilibrium Price and Quantity," January 3, 2015, https://www.youtube.com/watch?v=7eZcPs9z9OA.
7. Hayek, F. A. "The Use of Knowledge in Society." *The American Economic Review* 35, no. 4 (1945): 519–30. http://www.jstor.org/stable/1809376.
8. Dsouza Prabhu, Ruth, ed. *India's Most Legendary Restaurants*. New Delhi: Aleph Book Company, 2024.
9. "HET: The Socialist Calculation Debate," n.d. https://www.hetwebsite.net/het/essays/paretian/socialcalc.htm.
10. Government of India. *THE ESSENTIAL COMMODITIES ACT, 1955*, 1955. https://dfpd.gov.in/WriteReadData/Other/act5.pdf.

11. PRS Legislative Research. "The Essential Commodities (Amendment) Bill, 2020," n.d. https://prsindia.org/billtrack/the-essential-commodities-amendment-bill-2020.
12. Press Trust of India. "NPPA Fixes Price Caps for 12 Anti-diabetic Medicines." The *Economic Times*, October 25, 2021. https://economictimes.indiatimes.com/industry/healthcare/biotech/pharmaceuticals/nppa-fixes-price-caps-for-12-anti-diabetic-medicines/articleshow/87258088.cms.
13. Sharma, Priyanka. "India Caps Prices of 53 Drug Combinations, Including Tablets for Diabetes and Heart Disease." *Mint*, March 8, 2025. https://www.livemint.com/industry/drug-combinations-drug-price-control-diabetes-tablets-heart-disease-respiratory-diseases-depression-drugmakers-11741343900312.html.
14. Kaul, Rhythma. "Govt Caps Coronary Stent Price at Rs 30,000 in Relief for Lakhs of Patients | Latest News India." *Hindustan Times*, February 14, 2017. https://www.hindustantimes.com/india-news/in-a-relief-to-lakhs-of-patients-govt-caps-coronary-stent-price/story-WfmpwOUxvvWoSiTW7hoBEO.html.
15. Tabarrok, Alex. "The Lesson of the Spoons." Marginal Revolution (blog), August 13, 2019. https://marginalrevolution.com/marginalrevolution/2019/08/spoons-are-in-aisle-9.html.
16. Bhagwati, Jagdish, and Arvind Panagariya. "Rural inefficiency act: Despite protests about diluting NREGA, the PM is right to confine it to 200 poorest districts." The *Times of India* (blog), October 23, 2014. https://timesofindia.indiatimes.com/blogs/toi-edit-page/rural-inefficiency-act-despite-protests-about-diluting-nrega-the-pm-is-right-to-confine-it-to-200-poorest-districts/.

17. Open Learning. "Economics Explains Discrimination in the Labour Market," n.d. https://www.open.edu/openlearn/society-politics-law/economics/economics-explains-discrimination-the-labour-market/content-section-5.2.

CHAPTER 4: WHY DO THINGS KEEP GETTING MORE EXPENSIVE?

1. Menger, Carl. "On The Origin of Money." *The Economic Journal* 2, no. 6 (June 1, 1892): 239-255. https://doi.org/10.2307/2956146.
2. Burdett, Kenneth, Alberto Trejos, and Randall Wright. "Cigarette Money." *Journal of Economic Theory* 99, no. 1–2 (July 1, 2001): 117–42. https://doi.org/10.1006/jeth.2000.2731.
3. Hordijk, Wim. "From Salt to Salary: Linguists Take a Page From Science." *NPR*, November 8, 2014. https://www.npr.org/sections/13.7/2014/11/08/362478685/from-salt-to-salary-linguists-take-a-page-from-science.
4. Hanke, Steve H., and Erik Bostrom. "Zimbabwe Hyperinflates, Again: The 58th Episode of Hyperinflation in History." Studies in Applied Economics, no. 90. Johns Hopkins University Institute for Applied Economics, Global Health, and the Study of Business Enterprise, October 2017.
5. Martin, Marina B.V. "An Economic History of Hundi, 1858–1978." PhD diss., London School of Economics and Political Science, 2012.
6. Madras Courier. "From Coins & Hundi to Bank Notes: The Evolution of Currency in India." May 22, 2023. https://madrascourier.com/insight/from-coins-hundi-to-bank-notes-the-evolution-of-currency-in-india/.
7. Reserve Bank of India. "Early Issues." Accessed February 17, 2026. https://www.rbi.org.in/commonman/english/Currency/Scripts/Ear-

lyIssues.aspx.

8. Friedman, Milton, and Anna J. Schwartz. *A Monetary History of the United States, 1867–1960*. Princeton: Princeton University Press, 1963.
9. Soltani, Ehsan. "Money Supply Growth in Major Economies (2019–2023)." *Voronoi*. February 18, 2024. Accessed February 17, 2026. https://www.voronoiapp.com/economy/Money-Supply-Growth-in-Major-Economies-20192023-688
10. Bhardwaj, Ankur. 2021. *Covid-19 and Policy: How Nations Responded to the Challenge*. Centre for Economic Data and Analysis (CEDA), Ashoka University. Published on ceda.ashoka.edu.in.
11. Sierra, Gabrielle, host. "The Dollar Privilege." *Why It Matters*. Podcast. Council on Foreign Relations. February 18, 2021. https://www.cfr.org/podcasts/why-it-matters/dollar-privilege
12. International Monetary Fund. "Should Monetary Finance Remain Taboo?" IMF Blog, February 22, 2022. https://www.imf.org/en/Blogs/Articles/2022/02/22/should-monetary-finance-remain-taboo.
13. Hayek, Friedrich A. *Prices and Production*. London: George Routledge & Sons, 1931.
14. Oppers, Stefan Erik. "The Austrian Theory of Business Cycles: Old Lessons for Modern Economic Policy?" IMF Working Paper WP/02/2. International Monetary Fund, January 2002. https://www.imf.org/en/Publications/WP/Issues/2016/12/30/The-Austrian-Theory-of-Business-Cycles-Old-Lessons-for-Modern-Economic-Policy-15480.

CHAPTER 5: WHY DO SOME COUNTRIES GET RICH WHILE OTHERS STAY POOR?

1. Dubey, Vivek. "India's Vehicle Sales Crash 7% in Feb 2025, Rural

Demand Outpaces Cities: FADA." *CNBC TV18*, March 6, 2025. Accessed April 14, 2025. https://www.cnbctv18.com/auto/indias-vehicle-sales-crash-7-in-feb-2025-rural-demand-outpaces-cities-fada-19569623.htm

2. The *Economist*. "Our Big Mac Index Shows How Burger Prices Differ across Borders." The *Economist*. Accessed February 14, 2026. https://www.economist.com/interactive/big-mac-index
3. Sen, Amartya. "Development as Capability Expansion." *Journal of Development Planning* 19 (1989): 41–58.
4. Oxford Poverty & Human Development Initiative. "Gross National Happiness." Oxford Poverty & Human Development Initiative (OPHI), accessed February 14, 2026. https://ophi.org.uk/gross-national-happiness
5. Lucas, Robert E., Jr. 1988. "On the Mechanics of Economic Development." *Journal of Monetary Economics* 22 (1): 3–42.
6. Simon, Julian L. *The Ultimate Resource*. Princeton, NJ: Princeton University Press, 1981.
7. Shah, Parth J. *Why Is India Poor?* Liberty & Society Series 1. New Delhi: Centre for Civil Society, 2013.
8. Ritchie, Hannah. "Who Would Have Won the Simon-Ehrlich Bet over Different Decades, and What Do Long-Term Prices Tell Us about Resource Scarcity?" *Our World in Data*, January 6, 2025. Accessed February 15, 2026. https://ourworldindata.org/simon-ehrlich-bet
9. Maddison, Angus. *The World Economy: Volume 1: A Millennial Perspective and Volume 2: Historical Statistics*. Paris: OECD Publishing, 2006.
10. Acemoglu, Daron, and James A. Robinson. *Why Nations Fail: The*

Origins of Power, Prosperity, and Poverty. New York: Crown Currency, 2012.

11. Rajan, Raghuram. "Assume Anarchy? Why an Orthodox Economic Model May Not Be the Best Guide for Policy." *Finance & Development*, vol. 41, no. 3 (September 2004): 56–57.
12. Royal Swedish Academy of Sciences. "The Prize in Economic Sciences 2025 – Press Release." Press release, October 13, 2025. Accessed February 22, 2026. https://www.nobelprize.org/prizes/economic-sciences/2025/press-release/.
13. Mokyr, Joel. *The Gifts of Athena: Historical Origins of the Knowledge Economy*. Princeton: Princeton University Press, 2002.
14. Mokyr, Joel. *A Culture of Growth: The Origins of the Modern Economy*. Princeton: Princeton University Press, 2016.
15. McCloskey, Deirdre Nansen. *Bourgeois Dignity: Why Economics Can't Explain the Modern World*. Chicago: University of Chicago Press, 2010.
16. Henrich, Joseph. *The WEIRDest People in the World: How the West Became Psychologically Peculiar and Particularly Prosperous*. New York: Farrar, Straus and Giroux, 2020.

CHAPTER 6: WHY DO SOME PEOPLE GET RICH WHILE OTHERS STAY POOR?

1. Wani, Samreen. "Indian Companies Spend Less than 1% of Net Sales on R&D." *Forbes India*. August 4, 2025. https://www.forbesindia.com/article/news/indian-companies-spend-less-than-1-of-net-sales-on-rampd/96497/1
2. Bhandari, Bhupesh. "Once There Was the Bombay Club…." *Business Standard* (New Delhi), July 8, 2011. https://www.business-standard.com/article/opinion/bhupesh-bhandari-once-there-was-the-

bombay-club-111070800048_1.html

3. Patel, Deepak. "IndiGo Briefly Becomes World's Most Valuable Airline by Market Cap." *Business Standard*, April 9, 2025. https://www.business-standard.com/companies/news/indigo-turns-world-s-most-valuable-airline-m-cap-tops-delta-airlines-125040900742_1.html
4. Smith, Adam. *An Inquiry into the Nature and Causes of the Wealth of Nations*. London: W. Strahan and T. Cadell, 1776.
5. Bora, Garima. "How Licious Was Founded after a Messy Episode of Soan Papdi Packaging." The *Economic Times*. October 4, 2021. https://economictimes.indiatimes.com/small-biz/entrepreneurship/how-licious-was-founded-after-a-messy-episode-of-soan-papdi-packaging/articleshow/86745895.cms
6. McCloskey, Deirdre Nansen. *Bourgeois Dignity: Why Economics Can't Explain the Modern World*. Chicago: University of Chicago Press, 2010.
7. Mokyr, Joel. *The Gifts of Athena: Historical Origins of the Knowledge Economy*. Princeton: Princeton University Press, 2002.
8. Graham, Paul. "Mind the Gap." *paulgraham.com*. May 2004. Accessed February 23, 2026. https://paulgraham.com/gap.html
9. Graham, Paul. "Economic Inequality." *paulgraham.com*. January 2016. Accessed February 23, 2026. https://paulgraham.com/ineq.html
10. Nadh, Kailash. "Scaling with Common Sense #2: Being Future Ready." *Zerodha Tech Blog*. July 28, 2021. Accessed February 24, 2026. https://zerodha.tech/blog/being-future-ready-with-common-sense/
11. Milanovic, Branko. "Global income inequality in numbers: In his-

tory and now." *Global policy* 4, no. 2 (2013): 198-208.

12. Kuznets, Simon. "Economic Growth and Income Inequality." *American Economic Review* 45, no. 1 (March 1955): 1–28.
13. Riddell, Rebecca, Nabil Ahmed, Alex Maitland, Max Lawson, and Anjela Taneja. *Inequality Inc.: How Corporate Power Divides Our World and the Need for a New Era of Public Action*. Oxford: Oxfam International, January 2024.
14. de Soto, Hernando. *The Mystery of Capital: Why Capitalism Triumphs in the West and Fails Everywhere Else*. New York: Basic Books, 2000.

CHAPTER 7: WHAT HAPPENS WHEN POLITICS MEETS ECONOMICS?

1. Smith, Adam. *An Inquiry into the Nature and Causes of the Wealth of Nations*. London: W. Strahan and T. Cadell, 1776.
2. Friedman, Milton, and Rose Friedman. *Free to Choose: A Personal Statement*. New York: Harcourt Brace Jovanovich, 1980.
3. Buchanan, James M., and Gordon Tullock. *The Calculus of Consent: Logical Foundations of Constitutional Democracy*. Ann Arbor: University of Michigan Press, 1962.
4. Gelman, Andrew, Nate Silver, and Aaron Edlin. "What Is the Probability Your Vote Will Make a Difference?" Economic Inquiry 50, no. 2 (2012): 321–326.
5. Jain, Ritika, and Amit Nandan. "Electricity Prices and Firms' Decisions and Outcomes: The Case of India after a Decade of the Electricity Act." Energy Economics 91 (2020): 104915. https://doi.org/10.1016/j.eneco.2020.104915.
6. CNBCTV18.com. "Bike Taxi Ban in Karnataka: Ola, Uber, Rapido to Halt Services from June 16." CNBC-TV18, June 13, 2025. Accessed February 24, 2026. https://www.cnbctv18.com/india/karnataka-bike-

taxi-ban-ola-uber-rapido-june-16-high-court-order-19620749.htm.

7. Bopanna, Deepak. "Bike Taxi Ban Revoked in Karnataka, High Court Says Impose Conditions." NDTV, January 23, 2026. Accessed February 25, 2026. https://www.ndtv.com/india-news/bike-taxi-ban-revoked-in-karnataka-high-court-says-impose-conditions-10850967.
8. Raj, Sagay. "Over 5,000 Bike Taxi Riders Rally in Bengaluru Demanding Rollback of Ban." *India Today*. June 21, 2025. Accessed February 25, 2026. https://www.indiatoday.in/india/story/namma-bike-taxi-association-karnataka-ban-bengaluru-legal-framework-auto-unions-2744227-2025-06-21.
9. Joshi, Bharath. "Panel Asks Karnataka Government to Lift 33-Year Freeze on Permitting New Liquor Shops." *Deccan Herald*, February 5, 2025. https://www.deccanherald.com/india/karnataka/panel-asks-govt-to-lift-33-year-freeze-on-permitting-new-liquor-shops-3389554.
10. Henderson, David R. "Rent Seeking." In *The Concise Encyclopedia of Economics*. Carmel, IN: Liberty Fund, 2008. Accessed February 25, 2026. https://www.econlib.org/library/Enc/RentSeeking.html
11. Yandle, Bruce. "Bootleggers and Baptists—The Education of a Regulatory Economist." Regulation 7, no. 3 (1983): 12–16.
12. Mahalanobis, Prasanta Chandra. *Report of the Committee on Integration of Science with Agriculture*. New Delhi: Government of India Planning Commission, 1964.
13. Government of India. The Monopolies and Restrictive Trade Practices Act, 1969. No. 54 of 1969, § 5.
14. Kathuria, Sanjay. "Commercial Vehicles Industry in India: A Case History, 1928–1987." *Economic and Political Weekly* 22, no. 42/43 (1987): 1809–23. http://www.jstor.org/stable/4377638.
15. Government of India. *Competition Act, 2002*. No. 12 of 2003.

16. Hayek, F. A. *Law, Legislation, and Liberty*. Edited by Jeremy Shearmur. Vol. 19 of *The Collected Works of F. A. Hayek*. Chicago: University of Chicago Press, 2022.

CHAPTER 8: WHO SHOULD DO WHAT?

1. Demsetz, Harold. "Information and Efficiency: Another Viewpoint." *The journal of law and economics* 12, no. 1 (1969): 1-22.
2. Nilekani, Rohini. "Samaaj, Sarkaar, Bazaar." Samaaj, Sarkaar, Bazaar: A Citizen-First Approach. Self-published, 2022. https://www.samaajsarkaarbazaar.in.
3. Marx, Karl. Critique of the Gotha Programme. 1875. In Marx/Engels Selected Works, Volume 3, 13–30. Moscow: Progress Publishers, 1970.
4. Simple History. "The Great Leap Forward (1958–62)," January 25, 2020. https://www.youtube.com/watch?v=xWRhPf9Qzmw.
5. TED-Ed. "What Is the Tragedy of the Commons? - Nicholas Amendolare," November 21, 2017. https://www.youtube.com/watch?v=CxC161GvMPc.
6. Bay, Michael, dir. *Armageddon*. Starring Bruce Willis and Ben Affleck. Buena Vista Pictures, 1998.
7. Kumar, Akash. "A Case for Shutting Down BSNL." *Deccan Herald*, December 1, 2020. Accessed February 25, 2026. https://www.deccanherald.com/opinion/a-case-for-shutting-down-bsnl-921991.html
8. Bharathi, SP. 2020. "Meen kuzhambu for all: How a TN village shares a pond to harvest fish every year." *The News Minute*, August 8, 2020. Accessed February 25, 2026. https://www.thenewsminute.com/tamil-nadu/meen-kuzhambu-all-how-tn-village-shares-pond-harvest-fish-every-year-130340
9. Cardenas, Juan Camilo, and Rajiv Sethi. "Elinor Ostrom: Fighting

the Tragedy of the Commons." Books & Ideas. September 12, 2016. https://laviedesidees.fr/Elinor-Ostrom-Fighting-the-Tragedy-of-the-Commons.

10. Ostrom, Elinor. *Governing the Commons: The Evolution of Institutions for Collective Action*. Cambridge: Cambridge University Press, 1990.
11. Das, Gurcharan. *India Grows at Night: A Liberal Case for a Strong State*. New Delhi: Allen Lane, 2012.
12. Rajagopalan, Shruti, and Alexander Tabarrok. "Lessons from Gurgaon, India's Private City." In Cities and Private Planning: Property Rights, Entrepreneurship and Transaction Costs, edited by David Emanuel Andersson and Stefano Moroni, 199–231. Cheltenham: Edward Elgar, 2014.
13. Marginal Revolution University, "The Coase Theorem," March 18, 2015, https://www.youtube.com/watch?v=00HPak2RLlQ.
14. Rajagopalan, Shruti. "Opinion | Ronald Coase Has a Solution for Delhi's Air Pollution." *Mint*, November 11, 2019. https://www.livemint.com/opinion/columns/ronald-coase-has-a-solution-for-delhis-air-pollution-11573491626858.html.
15. Alt Carbon. "Mitsubishi Corporation & Alt Carbon Sign Agreement to Scale Carbon Removal in South Asia | Alt Carbon," March 12, 2025. https://www.alt-carbon.com/press-releases/mitsubishi-corporation-alt-carbon-sign-agreement-to-scale-carbon-removal-in-south-asia.
16. Tax Foundation. "Pigouvian Tax Definition | TaxEDU Glossary," February 8, 2024. https://taxfoundation.org/taxedu/glossary/pigouvian-tax/.
17. *Forbes*. "The Next Billion." *Forbes*, October 26, 2007. https://www.forbes.com/forbes/2007/1112/048.html.

18. *Fortune*. "How Yahoo! Won the Search Wars." *Fortune*, March 2, 1998. https://fortune.com/1998/03/02/how-yahoo-won-the-search-wars/.
19. Akerlof, George A. "The Market for 'Lemons': Quality Uncertainty and the Market Mechanism." *The Quarterly Journal of Economics* 84, no. 3 (1970): 488–500. https://doi.org/10.2307/1879431.
20. "SA8000 Standard & Walmart - SAI." SAI. Accessed September 9, 2025. https://sa-intl.org/resources/sa8000-and-walmart/
21. Ministry of Consumer Affairs, Food & Public Distribution. "Over 450 products under the ambit of mandatory certification." Press Information Bureau. August 2, 2022. https://www.pib.gov.in/PressReleasePage.aspx?PRID=1847501.
22. "The AI doctor will see you…eventually." The *Economist*, March 27, 2024. https://www.economist.com/leaders/2024/03/27/the-ai-doctor-will-see-youeventually.
23. Schwantes, Marcel. "Warren Buffett Says What Separates Successful People From Everyone Else Really Comes Down to a Two-Letter Word." Inc.com. November 12, 2021. https://www.inc.com/marcel-schwantes/warren-buffett-says-what-separates-successful-people-from-everyone-else-really-comes-down-to-a-2-letter-word.html
24. Welch, Jack, and Suzy Welch. *Winning*. New York: Harper Business, 2005.
25. Pritchett, Lant. "Is India a Flailing State?: Detours on the Four Lane Highway to Modernization." HKS Faculty Research Working Paper Series RWP09-013. John F. Kennedy School of Government, Harvard University, 2009.

ACADEMIC TOPICS COVERED IN THIS BOOK

Introductory Microeconomics	Scarcity, opportunity cost, division of labour, voluntary exchange, supply and demand, price theory, consumer and producer surplus, market equilibrium, price control
Introductory Macroeconomics	GDP, inflation, money, monetary policy, fiscal policy
International Economics	Comparative advantage, gains from trade, tariffs, protectionism, PPP
Public Economics/ Public Finance	Public goods, externalities, taxation, government failure, public choice
Development Economics	Economic growth, institutions, inequality, poverty, convergence
Monetary Economics	Money supply, inflation theory, quantity theory, fiat currency, central banking
Labour Economics	Wage determination, discrimination, labour market distortions
Industrial Economics	Market power, competition, innovation, creative destruction, regulation
Institutional Economics	Property rights, rules of the game, inclusive vs extractive institutions
Environmental Economics	Commons, Coase theorem, Pigouvian taxes, carbon markets
Indian Economy	Licence raj, liberalisation, MGNREGA, Essential Commodities Act, tariff policy, PSUs, regulatory landscape
Economists Referred to	Adam Smith, David Ricardo, Frederic Bastiat, Karl Marx, Friedrich Hayek, Milton Friedman, James Buchanan, Gordon Tullock, Gary Becker, George Akerlof, Ronald Coase, Arthur Pigou, Elinor Ostrom, Joseph Schumpeter, Daron Acemoglu, James Robinson, Joel Mokyr, Deirdre McCloskey, Joseph Henrich, Amartya Sen, Simon Kuznets, Branko Milanovic, Julian Simon, Raghuram Rajan, Jagdish Bhagwati, Arvind Panagariya, Lant Pritchett, Bruce Yandle, Alex Tabarrok, Shruti Rajagopalan and Hernando de Soto.